Armenian Family

Favorite Recipes

Aida Sarkisian

Copyright © 2011 Aida Sarkisian

All rights reserved.

ISBN: 0615465994

ISBN-13: 978-0615465999

In loving memory

of my mother Siranush.

CONTENTS

	Introduction	i
1	Appetizers	Pg 1
2	Salads	Pg 7
3	Soups and broths	Pg 13
4	Second course dishes:	Pg 21
	Meats, Poultry, Fish, Shellfish	
5	Miscellaneous	Pg 47
6	Pilafs	Pg 59
7	Savory pastries and pies	Pg 63
8	Breads	Pg 85
9	Desserts	Pg 91
10	Preserves	Pg 107
11	Useful advice and practical hints	Pg 117

INTRODUCTION

Food and its preparation are the essential parts of Armenian culture. Old Armenian recipes have been passed down from one generation to the next, from mother to daughter. Most recipes in this book have been passed down from my mother. There are also some international recipes along with my own.

Among my vivid childhood memories are the sweet smells and aromas coming from our kitchen, where my mother and grandmother were cooking. Over the years I decided to create a book to preserve my family's recipes.

Arranged by category, from appetizers to desserts, these recipes can bring more variety to everyday menus and add special flavors for family gathering and holiday events.

I was born and lived in Baku, a great city on the shore of the Caspian Sea. My family roots are from Karabakh, which is populated by Armenians and located between the Caspian Sea and the Black Sea.

My family and I have been residing in Vermont, United States since 1992.

1. APPETIZERS

MEAT STUFFED TRIANGLES

Dough:
½ cup sour cream, warm
2 egg yolks
¼ cup margarine, melted
Pinch of baking soda
Pinch of salt
2 ½ cup all-purpose flour

Filling:
¼ pound beef, cooked, ground
1 large onion, finely chopped
3 Tbsp sweet butter
1/3 cup pomegranate seeds
Salt and pepper to taste

For top brushing:
1 egg yolk, beaten

Mix baking soda with sour cream. Sift the flour over a bowl and add the sour cream mixture, egg yolks, margarine and salt. Mix from the center to the edges, using a large spoon, until well blended. On a lightly floured surface, knead dough until elastic and smooth. Cut into 3 pieces and shape into balls. Cover and let the dough rest for 30 minutes.
Meanwhile, in a heavy skillet heat the butter, add onions and fry over moderate heat until golden. Add the ground meat, salt, and pepper. Mix and fry for 1-2 minutes. Cool to room temperature. Add pomegranate seeds and mix. Roll out one ball into 15 inches in diameter dough sheet. Cut with a sharp knife into small squares. Put 1 teaspoon of filling into each square and pinch together the edges tightly. Do the same with the remaining balls. Brush the triangles with beaten egg and bake in preheated 325F oven for 15 minutes or until golden.
Serve warm or cooled.

BLACK AND RED CAVIAR BITES

3 Tbsp black caviar
3 Tbsp red caviar

2 Tbsp sweet unsalted butter
4 green onions, finely chopped
¼ pound wheat bread

Cut the bread into small, bite size squares. Spread the butter, top with caviar (black or red, separately) and sprinkle over chopped onions. Place on a flat serving plate and serve right away.

BEANS WITH FRIED ONIONS

1 cup pinto beans, boiled
2 medium onions, sliced into half rings
½ cup sunflower oil
1 Tbsp dried herbs (cilantro, dill, mint, basil)
Salt and pepper to taste

In a bowl slightly mash the beans.
In a heavy skillet heat the oil, add the onions and fry over moderate heat until soft.
Mix beans, onions, herbs, salt, and pepper. Toss well and pour into serving bowl.
Serve chilled with plain crackers.

BEAN SPREAD

1 cup pinto beans, boiled
½ cup walnuts
3 garlic cloves
1 tsp salt
3 twigs fresh cilantro, minced
¼ cup sweet butter, softened

Puree the beans, walnuts, and garlic in processor. Add the butter and salt. Mix well and transfer into serving bowl. Chill in refrigerator for one hour.
Before serving garnish with fresh cilantro.
Serve with plain crackers.

EGGPLANT CAVIAR

2 eggplants
1 green bell pepper
1 red bell pepper
4 medium tomatoes
1 large onion, finely chopped
3 twigs cilantro, minced
4 Tbsp olive oil
Salt and freshly ground black pepper to taste

Bake eggplants, peppers, tomatoes in a preheated 425F oven or over an open flame, turning several times, until cooked. Cool enough to handle. Peel off the skin, and put into the processor. Mash them lightly for a few seconds.
In a large skillet heat the olive oil, add the onions and fry over moderate heat until golden. Add eggplants, peppers and tomato mixture.
Bring to a boil. Stirring constantly, cook over moderate heat until all of the moisture in the skillet has evaporated. Add salt, black pepper, cilantro and cook for 2-3 minutes longer. Cool and pour into a serving plate.
Serve chilled with plain crackers.

BEEF LIVER PATE

1 pound beef liver
1 medium carrot, chopped
1 medium onion, chopped
3 twigs parsley
3 Tbsp sweet butter
1 bay leaf
1 Tbsp water
Salt to taste

Place the butter, carrots, onions, parsley, bay leaf, water in a saucepan. Cover and simmer for 15 minutes. Add the liver and cook over low heat for about 15 minutes.
Take out the bay leaf. While the mixture is still hot, grind it in a meat grinder. Add salt and the liquid from saucepan. Mix well. Spoon into a serving platter and refrigerate. Serve chilled with plain crackers.

CHICKEN LIVER PATE

1 pound chicken liver
1 onion, chopped
1 carrot, chopped
2 Tbsp sweet butter
3 twigs cilantro, chopped
3 twigs parsley, chopped
1 handful pecans
Salt and freshly ground black pepper to taste

In a saucepan place the butter, carrots, onions, parsley, and cilantro. Simmer for 15 minutes. Add the liver and simmer for another 15 minutes. While still hot, grind the mixture through a meat grinder. Also grind the pecans. Add the pecans, salt, pepper, and the remaining liquid into the liver mixture and mix well until blended. Spoon into a serving bowl and refrigerate.
Serve chilled with plain crackers.

BOILED GREEN BEANS

1 pound green beans
5 garlic gloves, mashed
1 Tbsp vinegar
4 cups water
1 tsp salt

Tie together 10-15 beans with any natural thread. Bring water to a boil and add the beans. Cook over moderate heat for 30 minutes or until tender. Take out the beans, remove the strings and place the beans in a serving platter. Spread garlic over the beans, and sprinkle salt and vinegar.
Serve cooled.

BOILED COW TONGUE

1 cow tongue
½ bunch parsley

1 onion, cut in half
5 black peppercorns
3 cloves garlic, pureed
1 tsp salt

Boil tongue on medium heat for 90 minutes. Take out and for 2-3 minutes leave in cold water. Quickly take off the skin.
In the broth of the tongue add parsley, onion and peppercorns. Put the tongue back into the broth. Boil for an hour.
Take the tongue out and while it is hot, slice into pieces. Salt the pieces spread over pureed garlic and put on a flat serving plate.
Serve hot or cool with mustard or horseradish.

FRIED EGGPLANTS

3 eggplants, sliced
3 garlic cloves, mashed
2 Tbsp apple cider vinegar
½ cup corn oil
3 Tbsp minced cilantro
Salt to taste

Heat the oil in a non-stick skillet over medium heat until just smoking. Add eggplants, fry on both sides.
Mix garlic, cilantro, salt and vinegar. Cover every slice of eggplant with the mixture and put on a flat serving plate.
Serve chilled.

2. SALADS

HERRING SALAD ("Herring under the coat")

1 pound herring, cleaned from bones, chopped
2 potatoes, cooked, grated
2 beets, cooked, grated
2 carrots, cooked, grated
1 onion, sliced
3 eggs, boiled, minced
½ pound mayonnaise mixed with 1tsp boiled and cooled water
Salt and pepper to taste

On a flat, large serving platter place a layer of potatoes and layer of onions, then spread a thin layer of mayonnaise. Over the onions layer the herring. Spread another thin layer of mayonnaise. Over the herring place a layer of carrots and a layer of beets. Sprinkle salt, and pepper. Spread another thin layer of mayonnaise. Layer the eggs. Then spread a thin layer of mayonnaise. Sprinkle hard boiled grated egg yolks over the top. Refrigerate for about 2 hours.
Before serving cut like a cake. Serve chilled.

FISH SALAD

1 herring, cleaned from bones
1 apple, grated
2 Tbsp soft unsalted butter
3 dill twigs, minced
3 scallions, finely chopped

Mix the herring and butter in processor. Transfer into a bowl, add apples and dill. Mix well.
Transfer into a small salad plate, cover and refrigerate.
Serve chilled. Garnish with scallions.

SALAD "Olivie"

1 chicken breast, cooked, cut into small cubes
3 eggs, hard- cooked, chopped
3 carrots, cooked, diced

1 potato, cooked, diced
2 cucumbers, diced
3 pickles, diced
½ bunch dill, minced
1 can of sweet peas
½ cup sour cream
½ cup mayonnaise
Salt and freshly ground black pepper to taste

In a large bowl mix all ingredients. Transfer into salad plate and refrigerate for 2 hours.
Serve chilled.

SALAD "Vinaigrette"

½ cup pinto beans, boiled
2 large beets, boiled, cut into small cubes
2 large carrots, boiled, cut into small cubes
1 potato, boiled, cut into small cubes
4 pickles, cut into small cubes
1 large onion, finely chopped
1 tsp mustard
½ cup sunflower oil
1/3 tsp black pepper
½ Tbsp salt

In a heavy frying pan heat the oil. When it is sizzling hot, add onions and fry over moderate heat until golden.
In a large bowl combine beans, beets, carrots, potatoes, pickles, mustard, salt and pepper. Add fried onions and toss well.
Refrigerate for 1 hour.
Transfer into salad a plate and serve chilled.

VEGETABLE SALAD

2 tomatoes, sliced
2 small cucumbers, sliced
2 small red onions, sliced

1 twig basil, minced
Salt and freshly ground black pepper to taste

In a bowl combine tomatoes, cucumbers, onions and basil. Add salt and pepper just before serving. Toss well and serve.

VEGETABLE SALAD WITH WALNUTS

1 carrot, grated
1 apple, grated
1 tomato, sliced
3 garlic cloves, minced
¼ cup walnuts, fried, chopped
3 twigs cilantro, finely chopped
2 Tbsp olive oil
Salt, ground pepper to taste

In a bowl combine together all ingredients, toss well and serve.

BEET SALAD

1 pound beets, boiled, grated
5 garlic cloves, minced
½ cup walnuts, minced
½ cup sour cream
Pinch of salt

In a bowl combine beets, garlic and walnuts. Add sour cream and salt. Mix thoroughly and refrigerate for 1 hour.
Transfer into a salad plate and serve chilled.

CARROT SALAD

1 pound carrots, grated
1/3 cup pine nuts
3 garlic cloves, minced
3 twigs parsley, chopped

In a bowl combine together all ingredients and toss well. Transfer into salad plate and drizzle the classical dressing over the salad. To make a dressing in a bowl mix 4 Tbsp olive oil, 1 Tbsp apple cider vinegar, 1 tsp freshly ground black pepper and 1tsp salt.
Serve chilled.

AVOCADO SALAD

1 avocado, cut into cubes
1 tomato, sliced
½ bunch scallions, chopped
¼ cup walnuts, chopped
1 Tbsp fresh orange juice
1 tsp lemon juice
Salt and hot cayenne pepper to taste

In a bowl combine all ingredients, toss well and transfer into a salad plate. Serve chilled.

PINEAPPLE SALAD

1 can of pineapple
1 chicken breast, cooked, cut
1 can of sweet corn
1/3 pound hard cheese
1 cup mayonnaise

On a flat dish layer the pineapple. Spread the mayonnaise. Over the pineapples layer the chicken. Spread the mayonnaise. Layer the corn, and spread more mayonnaise. Grate cheese right on top of the salad.

MANGO SALAD

2 mangos peeled, cut into small pieces
1 ripe pear, peeled, cut into small pieces
1 shallot onion, finely chopped
2 garlic cloves, minced

3 twigs cilantro, minced
Salt and ground hot cayenne pepper to taste

In a medium size bowl combine all of the ingredients together and toss well. Transfer into a salad plate.
Serve chilled.

ASPARAGUS SALAD

1 pound asparagus, cut at an angle
4 garlic cloves, minced
1 Tbsp lemon juice
1 tsp olive oil
½ tsp salt
3 cups water

In a medium size pot bring the water to a boil. Add the asparagus. Cook for 2-3 minutes, then drain.
In a bowl combine asparagus with other ingredients and toss well. Transfer into a salad plate and serve.

3. SOUPS AND BROTH

LAMB SOUP ("Pity")

2 pounds fatty lamb, cut into small pikes
2 pounds small yellow potatoes, pilled
½ pound yellow peas, soaked overnight
1 pound small onions, peeled
3 Tbsp salt
½ tsp freshly ground black pepper

For this dish it is very important to cook it in individual deep clay pots.

In the bottom of each pot place a few pikes of lamb, add 2 tablespoon peas, one whole potato, one whole onion, salt, and pepper to taste. Add water until covered. Put the pots into a preheated 325F oven for 2 hours. Serve hot with homemade fresh, crispy bread and marinated cucumbers.

LAMB SOUP ("Kyufta- Bozbash")

1 pound ground lamb
½ cup yellow peas, soaked overnight
1 onion, minced
1 large potato, cut into 4 pieces
1 large onion, finely chopped
1 egg
2 Tbsp sweet butter
1/3 pound sour prunes
½ bunch dill, chopped
2 twigs mint, minced
Pinch of saffron, soaked in one teaspoon hot water
Salt and freshly ground black pepper to taste
6 cups water

In a bowl mix well the lamb, minced onions, egg, dill, salt and pepper. In a pot melt the butter over medium heat. Add the chopped onions and saffron. Simmer for 5 minutes. Add the water and bring to a boil. Add peas and potatoes and cook for 10 minutes.
Divide the lamb mixture into equal portions. Shape them into small balls and drop carefully into the boiling soup. Add prunes and salt. Cook for 25 minutes. Garnish with mint.

VEGETABLE SOUP ("Borshch")

1 pound beef, cut into 1-inch chunks
1 large beet, cut into small cubes
2 carrots, cut into small cubes
1 large onion, cut into small cubes
2 tomatoes, without skin, chopped
1 potato, cut into small pieces
¼ pound cabbage, finely chopped
2 bay leaves
Salt and freshly ground black pepper to taste
6 cups water
½ cup sour cream

In a pot and over low heat cook the beef with 2 cups of water until tender. Drain the broth and set aside. In the same pot to the cooked meat add the onions, tomatoes, beets, and carrots. Cover and simmer for 10 minutes. Add the broth, remaining water and cook over moderate heat for 10 minutes.. Bring to a boil and add the potatoes, then cook for 10 minutes.
Add cabbage, bay leafs, salt and pepper. Cook partially covered for 10 more minutes. Remove the soup from heat. Cover and let stand for 10 minutes.
Serve hot with sour cream aside.

HERB SOUP ("Green Borsch")

1 onion, finely chopped
1 potato, diced
½ bunch parsley, chopped
½ bunch dill, chopped
1 bunch scallions, chopped
1 bunch spinach, chopped
1 bunch sorrel, chopped
5 Tbsp sweet butter
1 egg beaten
5 cups water
Salt and freshly ground black pepper to taste
½ cup sour cream

In a deep pot sauté the onions with butter for 10 minutes. Add the water and bring to a boil. Add the potatoes, all of the chopped herbs, salt and pepper. Cook for 15-20 minutes and drizzle in the beaten egg, stirring constantly. Remove from the heat, cover and let stand for 10 minutes. Serve hot with sour cream.

CHICKEN SOUP

½ pound chicken, cut into small chunks
1 onion, finely chopped
1 carrot, finely chopped
1 handful of angel hair pasta
3 twigs dill, minced
1 tsp dried herbs (cilantro, mint)
Salt and pepper to taste
3 cups water

In a cooking pot sauté the chicken and the onions for 5-6 minutes. Add the water and bring to a boil. Add carrots, salt, pepper and cook over low heat for 15 minutes.
Add the pasta and cook for another 15 minutes. Sprinkle dried herbs and then tightly cover the pot and remove from the heat.
Let stand for 10 minutes. Serve hot.

BEET SOUP ("Svekolnik")

3 beets, half cooked, diced
2 onions, diced
2 tomatoes, peeled, sliced
1 tsp lemon juice
1 tsp salt
½ tsp hot cayenne pepper
4 cups water
½ cup sour cream

In a cooking pot bring the water to boil. Add onions, tomatoes, beets, salt and pepper and cook over moderate heat for 20 minutes. Remove from the heat, add lemon juice, cover and let it sit for 30 minutes. Serve cold or hot with sour cream aside.

LENTIL SOUP

1 cup lentils, washed
1 onion, finely chopped
1 carrot, finely chopped
2 garlic cloves, minced
3 Tbsp sweet butter
1 Tbsp dried herbs (cilantro, parsley)
Salt and pepper to taste
4 cups water

In a large saucepan sauté the onions and garlic in butter. Add the carrots and cook for 3-5 minutes over moderate heat. Add the water and bring to a boil. Add lentils and cook over low heat until ready.
Sprinkle dried herbs and add salt and pepper. Mix well. Remove from the heat.
Serve hot with warm bread.

BEAN SOUP

1 cup brown beans, soaked overnight
1 onion, finely chopped
3 tbsp sweet butter
1/4 cup walnuts, chopped
2 cups water
Pinch of dried herbs (cilantro, mint)
Salt to taste

In cooking pot boil the water and add beans and cook until tender. Mash the beans lightly.
In a nonstick skillet heat the butter, add onions and fry over moderate heat until golden. Add the onion to the beans. Bring to a boil and add the walnuts, herbs and salt. Cook over low heat for 15 minutes. Cover and remove from the heat.
Serve hot with homemade crispy bread.

YOGURT SOUP ("Tanov")

This soup is one of Karabakh Armenians' favorite dishes.

1 pound plain yogurt
1 egg
1 Tbsp flour
½ bunch mint, minced
½ bunch chervil, minced
2 twigs cilantro, minced
1/3 cup rice or bulgur
5 cups water

In a deep cooking pot mix yogurt with flour and egg. Add the water, herbs and rice. Mix well and place over the high heat. Stirring constantly, bring to boil. Reduce the heat to low and stir until rice is tender.
Serve hot or chilled.

YOGURT AND CUCUMBER SOUP

2 cups plain yogurt
3 medium cucumbers, peeled, chopped
2 Tbsp finely chopped cilantro
½ tsp salt
1 tsp sugar
1 cup cold water

In a bowl mix the yogurt, sugar and salt until smooth. Add water and blend. Add cucumbers and cilantro. Pour into deep serving platter.
Serve chilled.

CHICKEN BROTH ("Bullion")

1 pound chicken thighs
½ pound chicken stomachs and hearts
1 large onion, cut in half
1 carrot
5 peppercorns

4 cups water
Salt to taste

Place chicken, stomachs and hearts in a large pot. Add water and over high heat bring to boil. Skim of the foam and scum from the top. Reduce the heat to low and add onions, carrots and peppercorns. Cook for 1 hour. Add salt.
Lay double layered wet cheesecloth in the strainer. Strain broth through a strainer in another pot. Use the meat and stock as needed.
Option: Serve hot chicken broth in large serving cups especially for bullions with the meat or chicken stuffed pastries ("Piroshkies").

BEEF BROTH ("Bullion")

1 pound beef
1 pound beef bones
1 large onion cut in half
2 celery sticks
1 bay leaf
1 parsley root
5 peppercorns
¼ bunch dill
5 cups water
Salt to taste

In a large cooking pot cook all ingredients over very low heat for about 2 hours. Lay double layered wet cheesecloth in the strainer. Strain broth through a strainer in another pot. Use the broth for soups or serve hot in special serving cups with crispy bread or crackers.

MEATBALL SOUP

1 pound ground beef
1 egg
1 onion, finely chopped
¼ cup rice
3 twigs cilantro, minced
Pinch of dried herbs

Salt and pepper to taste
4 cups water

In a bowl mix the meat, onions, egg, dried herbs, salt, and pepper.
In a cooking pot bring water to boil. Add rice, salt and stir well. Make small balls of meat mixture and carefully drop them into boiling water, one at a time. Cook over the moderate heat until rice is completely cooked and meatballs are floating on the top.
Sprinkle cilantro and serve hot.

COW FEET SOUP ("Khash")

6 pounds of clean cow feet
20 garlic cloves, peeled, pureed
1 cup pomegranate seeds
¼ cup wine vinegar
Salt to taste
12 cups water

In a large deep nonstick pot place the cow feet and pour the water. Bring to boil. Reduce the heat to medium and cook for 15 minutes. Take off foam which is rising on surface. Reduce the heat, as much as possible, to very low and cook overnight for several hours (for example, from 1a.m. to 7a.m.) until all bones come off the meat. Strain into a large bowl and remove the meat from the bones.
Pour the liquid back into the pot and add the meat. Bring to boil for a few minutes and remove from the heat.
Early in the morning instead of regular breakfast have this delicious soup with garlic, salt, pomegranate seeds and vinegar. How to serve?
In a bowl make a sauce mixing together garlic, pinch of salt and a few spoons of soup. Place on the table. Also put on the table pomegranate seeds, vinegar, salt and firm wheat bread or thin bread. Ladle the hot soup and a piece of meat into deep serving plates and serve individually. Spoon garlic sauce, pomegranate seeds, and vinegar into individual plates. Also add salt to taste, and soak a few chunks of wheat bread into the soup. Mix, eat and enjoy!

4. MEATS, POULTRY, FISH AND SHELFISH

POTTED BEEF ("Khazani khorovaz")

This dish is one of Karabakh Armenians classics.

2 pounds top quality beef, cut into 1 ½ -inch chunks
5 onions, cut in halves, thinly sliced
½ cup clarified butter
½ pound prunes
½ cup pomegranate seeds
1 bunch dill, minced
2 tsp salt
1 tsp freshly ground black pepper

In a heavy casserole melt one tablespoon butter. Wash the meat in cold water, squeeze and place to cook in casserole. Cook over the moderate heat, stirring occasionally, until the meat is tender, the water almost evaporated and meat starting to fry. Let it fry, stirring constantly, just for a few seconds. If the meat is not enough cooked add 3-4 prunes and half cup of hot water. Cover and cook longer until the meat is completely cooked. Reduce the heat to low, add salt and pepper, stir well and cover. Remove from the heat, set aside.
In a heavy skillet heat the remaining butter. Add onions and fry over the moderate heat, stirring frequently about 5 minutes. Add salt and pepper to taste. Add prunes and continue to fry until onions are golden on all sides. Add fried onions with prunes to the meat and mix well. Cover and simmer about 15 minutes, stirring only once. Transfer into a deep serving platter. Sprinkle with dill and over the dill sprinkle pomegranate seeds. Serve hot as a main dish.

BEEF STROGANOV ("Bef-Stroganov")

2 pounds high quality fillet of beef, trimmed of all fats
3 large onions, cut in half and thinly sliced
½ Tbsp powdered mustard
1 tsp sugar
4 Tbsp sunflower oil
3 Tbsp sour cream
Salt and freshly ground black pepper to taste
1 Tbsp hot water

In a small bowl mix together the mustard, sugar and pinch of salt. Add hot water, stir well and let stand for 15-20 minutes.

In a large heavy skillet heat 2 tablespoons oil and add the onions. Fry over the moderate heat, stirring constantly, until golden. Set aside.

Cut the meat into ¼ inches wide strips. Heat the remaining oil in another heavy skillet and drop in the meat strips, tossing constantly, and fry until they are lightly browned.

If the meat is not enough tender, cover the skillet and simmer for 10-15 minutes. Take off the lid, add fried onions, mustard paste, salt and pepper and fry together over the moderate heat, stirring constantly, for 2-3 minutes.

Add the sour cream, a tablespoon at a time, mix well, reduce the heat, cover and simmer for 3-5 minutes. Transfer the contents of the skillet to serving platter.

Serve hot.

POTTED BEEF LIVER

1 pound beef liver, cut into pieces
2 large onions, thinly sliced
½ cup prunes
½ bunch cilantro, minced
2 Tbsp sweet butter
1 tsp salt

In a middle size pot melt the butter, add onions, prunes and simmer for 10 minutes. Add the liver, cook over the medium heat for 10-12 minutes. Add salt and cilantro. Transfer the stew to a deep serving platter and serve hot.

PORK STEW

2 pounds pork, cut into small chunks
4 potatoes, peeled, cut
2 large onions , cut into small cubes
3 tomatoes, sliced
2 tsp salt
1/3 tsp freshly ground black pepper

Pinch of dried herbs
2 cups hot water

Wash the pork, put into the cooking pot, add the butter, cover and simmer for 10 minutes. Add the onions, tomatoes, one cup of hot water, cover, and cook over low heat until meat is almost cooked. Add the potatoes, the remaining water, salt, pepper and herbs and cook for 15 minutes. Remove from the heat, cover and let stand a few minutes. Serve hot.

MEATBALLS SIMMERED IN VEGETABLES

2 pounds ground meats (the combination of beef, pork and turkey)
1 large onion, finely chopped
3 large onions, sliced
1 egg
3 green bell peppers, sliced
1 red bell pepper, sliced
1 yellow bell pepper, sliced
5 tomatoes, sliced
½ cup sweet butter
1 Tbsp dried herbs
½ bunch cilantro, minced
Salt, pepper to taste

In a large bowl mix ground meat, chopped onions, egg, dried herbs, salt and pepper to taste. Mix well by hand, adding small portions of warm water until the mixture is well blended and smooth.
In a deep pan melt the butter, spread a layer of sliced onions, over it lay down peppers, the next layer place tomatoes and sprinkle salt and pepper. Take small portion of meat mixture, make a balls and place over the tomatoes. Put the remaining vegetables and meat in layers in the same order. Sprinkle salt and pepper.
Put inverted plate over, press and cook over the moderate heat for 10 minutes and then simmer for 30 minutes.
Transfer all to serving platter, sprinkle with cilantro.
 Serve hot.

GRAPEVINE LEAVES STUFFED WITH MEAT ("Dolma")

2 pounds high quality ground beef
2 large onions, finely chopped
½ cup rice, washed and drained
2 eggs
1Tbsp dried herbs (cilantro, basil, mint, dill)
2 Tbsp vodka
½ bunch fresh cilantro, finely chopped
½ bunch fresh mint, finely chopped
2 Tbsp sweet butter, melted
Salt and freshly ground black pepper to taste
1 pound fresh or marinated grape leaves
1 cup warm water

In a big bowl combine all ingredients, except water and grape leaves. Mix well by hand, adding warm water in small portions until the mixture is blended.
If using fresh grapevine leaves, soak them for 1 minute in hot water to soften them, then rinse under cold water. Squeeze them a little to take off access water. If using preserved grapevine leaves, rinse them with hot water, wash and drain.
Spread the leaves on a plate, stem end toward you, dull side up. Place one tablespoon (or less for smaller leaves) of the meat mixture near the stem ends. Fold the stem end over the stuffing, fold over the sides to enclose the stuffing, roll the grape leaf firmly away from you toward the tip, forming a cylinder.
Layer the stuffed leaves seam sides down in a pan, close together in neat rows, layer by layer and add little salted hot water over them until covered. Gently place inverted plate over the top to keep the stuffed leaves in place during cooking. Bring to a boil and cover. Lower the heat and simmer for 60 minutes. Turn off the heat, put over the lid a kitchen towel, let stand for 20 minutes. Transfer stuffed leaves carefully to a serving platter.
Serve hot with a small bowl of yogurt and garlic sauce (yogurt and crushed garlic) on the side.

ASSORTED STUFFED VEGETABLES

½ pound ground beef
½ pound ground pork
½ cup rice
2 eggs
2 onions, finely chopped
2 Tbsp vodka
½ bunch cilantro, minced
2 tsp flour
½ cup sweet butter
1 tsp freshly ground black pepper
4 small eggplants scoop out the pulp of each, leaving ¼ inch-thick shell all around and save to use later as covers.
3 apples cored
3 red bell peppers cut the tops and take out the seed
3 green bell peppers cut the tops and take out the seeds
4 firm tomatoes, cut the tops, scoop out the pulp and save to use later
Salt, pepper to taste
1/2 cup warm water for meat mixture
3 cups hot water for cooking

In a large bowl mix the meats, onions, eggs, rice, flour, vodka, cilantro, salt and pepper. Mix thoroughly, adding warm water in small portions until the mixture is well blended.
 Spoon the stuffing into vegetables and apples, place side by side in a deep cooking pot, cover with saved "lids", dot with sweet butter, sprinkle with salt and pepper and pour in hot water. Bring to boil and cover. Lower the heat and cook for 50 minutes.
Transfer carefully stuffed vegetables into a large oval shape serving platter and pour the pot juices over them.
Serve hot.

CABBAGE LEAVES STUFFED WITH MEAT

1 pound ground beef
1 pound ground pork
½ cup rice
2 eggs

3 onions finely chopped
2 Tbsp vodka or whisky
1 Tbsp flour
1 Tbsp dried herbs (cilantro, mint, basil, dill)
½ bunch fresh cilantro, finely chopped
½ bunch fresh dill, finely chopped
Pinch cayenne pepper
3 tsp salt
1 cup warm water
3 cups boiled water
10 prunes
1 quince, cut to 5-6 slices
2 apples, sliced
1/3 pound chestnuts, cleaned
4 tomatoes, sliced
3 pounds white cabbage

In a large bowl combine the meats, rice, onions, eggs, vodka, flour, dried and fresh herbs, salt and pepper. Mix thoroughly, adding from time to time small portions of warm water until the mixture is well blended. Prepare cabbage leaves. Remove core from cabbage. Carefully loosen the leaves. In a large pot boil the water, drop the cabbage leaves into the water for 5-6 minutes. Take the leaves from the water, cool them. Remove hard ribs from the leaves, divide the leaves in half if they are big and add 1 tablespoon of meat mixture. Fold over the sides and roll the leaf firmly, away from you. Make shape of a cylinder.
In a large saucepan place the stuffed leaves close together in rows. Between the layers put tomatoes, chestnuts, prunes, apples and quince and add salted boiling water. Gently place an inverted plate over the top, press lightly.
Cover and bring to boil. Reduce the heat to moderate and cook about an hour. Remove from heat, cover with a kitchen towel and set aside for 10-15 minutes.
Serve hot.

GRAPE LEAVES STUFFED WITH COTTAGE CHEESE

½ pound cottage cheese
1 Tbsp sour cream

½ cup raisins, washed
4 Tbsp sweet butter
15-20 fresh grape leaves, washed in hot water, squeezed
½ tsp salt

In a small bowl mix cottage cheese, sour cream and raisins. Put overturned grape leaves on a board and with a spoon slightly smash the hard parts of the veins. Put a small amount of cottage cheese mixture and roll like eggrolls. In a pan melt the butter and fry them slightly over the moderate heat on both sides.
Serve hot with crispy thin bread.

SHISH KEBAB ("Khorovaz")

One of the favorite Caucasian specialties- marinated broiled lamb or pork.

2 pounds lamb or pork, cut into 1½ -inches chunks
2 large onions, cut in half, thinly sliced
1tsp salt
½ tsp freshly ground black pepper

In a large bowl mix the onions, salt, and pepper. Add meat (never wash meat for shish kebab!) and toss well. Cover and let stand in a refrigerator until the next day.
Remove the onions from the meat. Thread the meat on long skewers, leaving a few inches bare at each edge. Broil over natural wood charcoal, 4-5 inches from the heat, turning frequently until the meat has browned evenly on all sides. Push the meat from skewers onto a deep serving plate. Serve at once with broiled vegetables, like eggplants, tomatoes, finely chopped fresh onions, finely chopped cilantro, salt and pepper. When charcoal is very hot first broil the whole eggplants, putting them over the charcoal, turning them carefully until cooked. Place them into salted cold water, peel them and chop. String the tomatoes on the skewers, broil over charcoal, until cooked. Take them from the skewers, peel off the skin and chop. Chop fresh onions, cilantro and in a deep bowl mix the eggplants, tomatoes, onions, cilantro, add salt and pepper . (need 2 eggplants, 4 tomatoes, 1 onion and ½ bunch cilantro).

GROUND MEAT SHISH KEBAB ("Liulia-Kebab")

One of the favorite Caucasian specialties – seasoned and broiled ground meat.

For a Karabakh Armenian version this dish has to be made from ground lamb, sheep's kurdyuk and seasonings. This recipe is my own version of this dish.

1 pound ground beef
1 pound ground pork
1 purple onion, finely chopped
2 shallot onions, grated
½ cup pomegranate seeds
4 twigs parsley, minced
Salt and freshly ground black pepper to taste

In a large bowl combine the beef, pork, turkey, shallot onions, salt and pepper. Mix well. Cover and let it stand for 2 hours.
With hands dipped in cold water, form portions of meat mixture around wide skewers, making rolls 1-inch of diameter and 10 inches long. Broil over the natural wood charcoal about 15 minutes, turning on all sides (especially at the beginning of broiling).
Serve at once with pomegranate syrup (narsharab) or with salad, made from fresh finely chopped purple onions, fresh pomegranate seeds and fresh minced parsley aside.

FRIED LAMB INTESTINES ("Dzhiz-biz")

½ pound lamb liver cut into small pieces
½ pound lamb lungs cut into small pieces
2 lamb kidneys (divide, hold in salted water for 2 hours) cut into small pieces
½ pound lamb entrails, cleaned, cut into small pieces
1 large onion, finely chopped
Salt and pepper to taste

In a heavy casserole fry over the moderate heat the entrails, and then add the kidneys and lungs.

Fry for 10 minutes. Add the liver and fry for 5 minutes. Add the onions, salt and pepper. Fry for 15 minutes more, stirring constantly, until the onions are golden brown.
Serve at once.

FRIED MEAT FILLETS

2 pound fillets of pork or beef, trimmed of fat and gristle
3 Tbsp clarified butter
½ tsp freshly ground black pepper
½ tsp freshly ground nutmeg
Salt to taste

Cut the meat into thin slices and sprinkle with salt, pepper and nutmeg. Cover with clear plastic and pound with a mallet until thin.
In a skillet heat the clarified butter. Add the meat and fry over the moderately slow heat to brown evenly, on both sides, until tender.
Serve hot with fresh vegetable salad.

FRIED MEAT WITH POTATOES

2 pounds beef or pork cut into 2-inch chunks
2 pounds middle size potatoes, peeled
1 cup clarified butter
2 tsp salt
½ tsp pepper

Wash the meat in cold water, squeeze slightly. In a heavy casserole heat one tablespoon of butter and add the meat. Cook over the moderately low heat until the liquid has evaporated and the meat is tender. Let it fry, stirring constantly, for 1-2 minutes. (If the meat is not completely cooked add a little water and cook until the meat is tender and began to fry). Add salt and pepper. Remove from the heat. Cover.
Meanwhile in a deep pot heat the remaining butter. Add the salted whole potatoes and fry over the moderate heat until all sides are golden brown. Place the meat and potatoes into a large oval shape serving platter.
Serve hot.

KHINKALI

Dough:
3 cups sifted all-purpose flour
1 ½ cup lukewarm water
Topping:
1 pound boneless beef or lamb, ground
1 large onion, finely chopped
1 cup yogurt
5 garlic cloves
2 Tbsp sweet butter
Salt and freshly ground black pepper to taste

In a bowl mix the flour with a pinch of salt, make a well in the center and add the water. Knead thoroughly until firm dough is formed. Cover with a kitchen towel and let it rest for 30 minutes. Divide into 4 equal pieces. Shape the balls, cover with a clear plastic, put aside.
In a heavy skillet melt the butter over the moderate heat. Add the onions and sauté until soft but not browned, stirring frequently. Add the meat and cook until browned. Add salt and pepper. Cover and simmer for 30 minutes.
Make a garlic-yogurt sauce with a pinch of salt.
On a lightly floured surface roll out one part of dough as thin as possible. With a sharp knife cut it into diamond shape pieces. In a large pot bring to boil ½ gallon of water. Add a pinch of salt. Drop the diamond shape dough pieces (10-12 at a time) into the boiling water for a few minutes. When they are floating, take them out with slatted spoon and place into a serving platter. Spread the meat mixture over them and drizzle over a few spoons of yogurt mixture. Do the same with the remaining dough, meat and yogurt.
Serve at once.

MEAT STUFFED DUMPLING ("Pelmeni")

Dough:
1 Tbsp sweet butter
1½ cups warm water
½ tsp salt
3 cups all-purpose flour

Filling:
1/3 pound ground beef
1/3 pound ground pork
1 onion, ground
1 tsp salt
½ tsp freshly ground black pepper

Sift the flour over a bowl. Add melted butter, water and salt. Knead, sprinkling with additional flour if needed until smooth. Divide the dough into 3 equal parts, shaping each into a ball. Cover with a kitchen towel and let it rest for 20 minutes.
In a bowl combine beef, pork, onions, salt and pepper. Knead with the hands until well blended. Set aside.
On a lightly floured surface roll out one ball until thin. Using a small glass cut into 1 ½ -inch in diameter small circles. Put ½ teaspoon filling and pinch the edges to seal. Bring the two outer corners together, pinching firmly.
 Repeat with the remaining balls of dough and the remaining filling. Drop the dumplings into the slightly salted boiling water and cook over the moderate heat about 10 minutes or until they are floating. Take them with slatted spoon from the water, place into a serving plate.
Serve at once with sour cream aside.

BEEF SIMMERED IN BEER

2 pounds beef cut into 1-inch chunks
3 Tbsp olive oil
1 large onion, sliced
1 cup beer
3 sticks celery, chopped
3 carrots, chopped
1 tsp honey
2 bay leaves
2 dill twigs, chopped
Salt and pepper to taste

In a saucepan sauté the onions in the oil and add the meat. Pour honey and fry a few minutes. Pour the beer and bring to a boil. Add carrots, celery, bay leaves, salt and pepper.

Reduce the heat to low, then simmer partially covered for 40 minutes or until the meat is tender. Transfer into deep serving platter and garnish with chopped dill.
Serve hot.

PORK IN RED WINE

2 pounds boneless lean loin pork, cut into small pieces
½ cup red wine
1 large onion, sliced
3 celery sticks, finely chopped
1 large tomato, skinned, sliced
5 garlic gloves, chopped
1 red bell pepper, sliced in strips
1 Tbsp olive oil
2 tsp brown sugar
Pinch of nutmeg
Pinch of hot cayenne pepper
½ bunch scallions, finely chopped
Salt to taste

In a heavy saucepan heat the oil. Add sugar. Stir well. Add meat and sauté quickly, until it turns brown. Add wine and nutmeg. Cook covered for 40 minutes.
 Add red peppers, celery, onions, garlic, tomatoes, cayenne pepper and salt. Cover and cook over the low heat 20 minutes more.
Serve hot in a deep serving platter. Sprinkle chopped scallions over the dish.

BEEF CUTLETS

2 pounds top quality beef, processed through a meat grinder
1 onion, processed with meat through the meat grinder
1 egg
1 slice soaked and squeezed wheat bread
3 Tbsp clarified butter
2 tsp dried herbs
Salt and pepper to taste

Combine the meat, onion, egg, bread, herbs, salt and pepper in a deep bowl. Knead well until thoroughly blended. With hands moistened in water shape the mixture into round patties about 2 inches in diameter and form into egg shaped ovals. Flatten them and fry in a heavy skillet in heated clarified butter over moderate heat until evenly brown on both sides.
Serve hot with fresh vegetable salad.

MEAT WITH CONVERTED WHEAT ("Kurkut")

2 pounds beef or pork, cut into 1 ½-inch chunks
3 cups hard wheat, converted or cracked
½ cup sweet butter (if meat is lean)
1 Tbsp salt
9 cups water

Into a large nonstick pot place one layer of meat. Sprinkle it with half of the wheat. Place another layer of meat and sprinkle it with the rest of the wheat. Add butter, salt and water. Don't mix! Bring to a boil over the moderate heat. Reduce the heat to very low, cover loosely; cook overnight (for example, from 1 a.m. to 7 a.m.) until most of the water has evaporated and the meat and wheat are tender.
Serve hot. Armenians serve "Kurkut" early in the morning as breakfast.

GROUND BEEF WITH MACARONI

1 pound macaroni
½ pound beef, cooked and ground
2 large onions, finely chopped
2 Tbsp sweet butter
Salt and pepper to taste

In a large pot bring the water to a boil. Add salt and macaroni. Cook until tender. Drain.
In a casserole heat the butter, add onions and fry over the moderate heat until golden.
Add ground meat to the onions and stirring frequently fry about 6-7 minutes. Add macaroni, salt, pepper and mix well. Serve hot.

STUFFED CHICKEN

1 whole chicken, washed
1 onion diced
2 Tbsp sweet butter, melted
1/3 cup raisins
3 dried apricots, finely chopped
3 prunes, finely chopped
1/3 cup rice, almost cooked
1 Tbsp dried herbs
1 Tbsp mayonnaise
Salt and pepper to taste

Dry the chicken inside and out with a paper towel.
In a bowl, mix rice, butter, onions, prunes, apricots, raisins, herbs, salt, and pepper. Loosely fill the body cavity with the stuffing. Tie the legs. Brush the chicken thoroughly with mayonnaise.
Line up a shallow baking sheet with aluminum foil. Place the chicken side up in the middle of the foil and put the leftover stuffing around the chicken.
Fold the foil over the stuffing and bake in preheated 350F oven an hour or until thoroughly cooked, depends on the size of the chicken.
Slightly cool the chicken, take the stuffing out. Carve the chicken and place into a large serving platter. Place the stuffing around it.
Serve hot with marinated garlic and pickles aside.

CHICKEN CUTLETS ("Cutlets po-Kievski")

4 skinless chicken breasts
2 eggs, beaten
4 Tbsp sweet butter
4 Tbsp clarified butter
5 twigs fresh cilantro, minced
2 twigs fresh dill, minced
1 tsp salt
½ tsp freshly ground black pepper
3 Tbsp plain bread crumbs

Combine sweet butter, cilantro and dill, mix and form oval shaped sticks.

Refrigerate until hardened.
Rub the chicken breasts with salt, pepper and pound them with a mallet, until thin and flat. Divide them into equal pieces. Put into every piece a portion of butter mix and roll. In a heavy skillet heat the clarified butter. Dump the chicken rolls into the beaten eggs, roll in the bread crumbs, dump again into the eggs, and roll in bread crumbs. Fry the cutlets in clarified butter until evenly browned on all sides.
Serve hot.

PRESSED FRIED CHICKEN ("Tapaka")

2 young chickens or Cornish game hens
6 garlic cloves, pureed
2 Tbsp sour cream
5 Tbsp clarified butter
1 tsp apple cider vinegar
2 tsp salt
½ tsp freshly ground black pepper
3 Tbsp water

Pat the chickens thoroughly dry with paper towels.
Beginning from the neck's end cut each bird lengthwise along the backbone. Discard the backbone. Cover the chickens with plastic or waxed paper and flatten by pounding with a cleaver. Rub with mixture of garlic, salt and pepper. Let stand in a cool place for 2-3 hours. Rub the inside of the chickens with sour cream. In a heavy skillet heat the butter over the moderate heat. Add the chickens. Set a heavy weight- such as another skillet laden with cans of food- on top of the chickens and cook about 10 minutes. Rub the skin side with sour cream, turn over, cover and cook under the press for 15 minutes. Reduce the heat, cook until deep golden brown.
Serve hot with sauce (pureed garlic, vinegar, water) on the side.

CHICKEN IN WHITE WINE

2 chicken breasts cut into peaces
2 Tbsp olive oil
2 zucchinis, sliced

1 red bell pepper, sliced
1 green bell pepper, sliced
1 teaspoon salt
½ teaspoon freshly ground black pepper
3 twigs of basil, minced
½ cup of white wine
3 garlic cloves, finely chopped
½ cup cheddar cheese
Salt and freshly ground black pepper to taste

In a roasting pan put zucchinis, chicken, red pepper and green pepper. Sprinkle with salt and pepper. Add garlic, basil, olive oil, wine.
On top of everything grate the cheese. Roast in the preheated 325F oven for 45 minutes.
Serve hot with pasta or rice aside.

CHICKEN STEW

1 whole chicken, cut into pieces
2 onions, cut into half rings
4 large tomatoes, peeled and sliced
1 Tbsp olive oil
2 bay leaves
3 twigs cilantro, minced
1 tsp salt
Pinch of cayenne pepper

In a deep, heavy skillet heat the oil. Fry the chicken over the medium heat for 10 minutes. Add onions, tomatoes, bay leaves, salt and pepper and stirring frequently cook for 15 minutes. Lower the heat, cover and simmer for 15 minutes. Transfer into a serving platter and garnish with cilantro.
Serve hot with warm, crispy bread.

CHICKEN WITH VEGETABLES ('"Chokhakhbeli")

1 chicken, cut into pieces
3 large onions, sliced
3 large tomatoes, peeled and sliced

2 bay leaves
1 tsp fresh grounded coriander seeds
2 Tbsp sweet butter
3 twigs fresh cilantro, minced
Pinch of cayenne pepper
Salt to taste

In a large heavy skillet heat the butter over the medium heat. Add the chicken. Sauté for 20 minutes. Add the onions and cook for 15 minutes, stirring frequently. Add the tomatoes, bay leaves, coriander, salt, and pepper. Mix well. Reduce the heat to low. Cover and simmer until the chicken is completely cooked.
Serve hot. Garnish with fresh cilantro.

TURKEY IN WALNUT SAUCE ("Satzivi")

1 whole small turkey
1 ½ pounds walnut
5 large onions, finely chopped
2 Tbsp olive oil
½ cup corn flour
1 head of garlic, cleaned and pureed
2 tsp freshly ground coriander seeds
Pinch of saffron
Freshly ground Georgian spice "Khmeli-Suneli".
½ tsp cayenne pepper
2 Tbsp vinegar
Salt to taste

Cook the entire turkey until half cooked. Take out of the broth, sprinkle salt, and bake in the oven at 320F for about 2 hours.
In a heavy skillet, heat olive oil, add the onions and fry over the heat until golden brown. Add the walnuts and two tablespoons of turkey broth. Cool and grind in a food processor. To the mixture add corn flour, garlic, coriander, saffron, khmeli-suneli, salt and pepper. Add ½ cup of broth to end up with a thick mixture.
In a heavy pan warm the turkey broth and add the mixture. Stirring slowly, bring to a boil. Boil for 5 minutes. Cool to room temperature and add vinegar. Mix well. Carve the turkey and put into the pan with the

mixture. Remove from the heat. Transfer "Satzivi" into a large serving platter.
Serve warm or cool.

CHICKEN BREAST ROLLS

2 chicken breasts
4 garlic cloves, minced
3 dill twigs, minced
½ bunch cilantro, minced
1 bell red pepper, thinly sliced in strips
1 bell yellow pepper, thinly sliced in strips
1 bell green pepper, thinly sliced in strips
2 large tomatoes, peeled, sliced
3 Tbsp olive oil
1 tsp salt
½ tsp freshly ground black pepper

Cover chicken breasts by plastic, pound slightly with mallet to flatten. With sharp knife divide the breasts in half. Put into each slice mixed dill, cilantro, garlic, salt, pepper and roll. Fix with toothpicks. Over the moderate heat in a skillet heat one tablespoon olive oil, sprinkle salt and pepper over the rolls and fry until golden brown. Put aside.
Into the same skillet add olive oil, fry peppers. Sprinkle salt and black pepper. Put aside. Fry tomatoes in the same skillet and add chicken rolls into tomatoes. Add little salt and pepper. Cook for 5 minutes. Serve with pasta or cooked rice. In one side of serving platter place pasta or rice, on the sides place chicken rolls and fried peppers. Pour cooked tomatoes over the pasta or rice and over the tomatoes sprinkle minced cilantro.

FRIED CHICKEN BREAST

2 chicken breasts, cut in the middle, make a pocket
6 gloves garlic, finally chopped
1 Tbsp mustard
1 tsp freshly squeezed lemon juice
2 Tbsp olive oil
3 Tbsp sweet butter

1 green apple, sliced into straw strips
1 sweet red pepper, thinly sliced in strips
A few twigs of fresh dill, cilantro and mint, minced
1 tsp salt
Pinch of cayenne pepper and freshly ground black pepper

Mix cilantro, garlic and dill. Fill the chicken pockets with herb mix. Close tightly.
In a bowl mix lemon juice, olive oil, mustard and rub the breasts.
In a nonstick skillet heat the butter. Add the breasts and fry over the moderate heat until cooked and both sides are golden brown. Transfer into a flat serving platter. Serve hot with sliced pepper and apple strips aside. Garnish with mint and dill.

CHICKEN BAKED IN WINE

2 chicken breasts cut into 6 triangles
6 gloves garlic, finally chopped
1 lemons zest
2 Tbsp lemon juice
½ cup white wine
1 Tbsp olive oil
½ cup pistachios, cracked
½ bunch cress salad, minced
½ bunch cilantro
Salt and pepper to taste

Pour olive oil into baking pan. Add, garlic, lemon zest, chicken and sprinkle salt and pepper. Put into preheated 325F oven and bake for 30 minutes. Over it pour lemon juice, wine and bake for 20 minutes more. Transfer into a serving platter. Serve hot. As a side dish serve mixed cilantro, pistachios, salt and pepper.

CHICKEN FRIED WITH PINEAPPLE

1 whole chicken, cut, bone removed
2 large onions, thinly sliced
1 pineapple, peeled, sliced

1 small piece of fresh ginger root, sliced
1 yellow bell pepper, sliced into strips
1 red bell pepper sliced into strips
1 green bell pepper, sliced into strips
3 twigs cilantro, minced
2 Tbsp olive oil
2 tsp salt
½ tsp freshly ground black pepper

In a heavy skillet heat the olive oil and add the onions. Fry over the moderate heat, stirring frequently, until golden. Add the peppers, pineapples and ginger. Fry for 5 minutes. Add chicken, salt and pepper and cook for 30 minutes. Transfer into a deep serving platter. Sprinkle with minced cilantro.
Serve hot.

MARINATED CHICKEN AND PORK

2 chicken breasts, sliced
1 pound pork, sliced
1/3 cup olive oil
¼ cup red wine
6 garlic cloves, pureed
3 twigs thyme
½ cup pomegranate's seeds
1 head lettuce
2 tbsp salt
1 tsp freshly ground black pepper

In a bowl mix olive oil, wine, garlic, thyme leaves, salt and pepper. Put into this marinade pork and chicken and leave overnight in a refrigerator.
Clear the chicken and pork from the leaves, grill them until golden brown. Serve hot with chopped lettuce and pomegranate seeds aside.

GOOSE ROASTED WITH APPLES

1 middle size goose, free of excess fat
2 apples, cored and quartered

1 large onion, quartered
½ cup rice, half cooked
1 tbsp olive oil
A few apricots
A few prunes
½ cup raisins
2 tsp salt
1 tsp freshly ground black pepper

Dry the goose thoroughly with paper towels. Salt and pepper the entire goose. Mix rice with olive oil in a bowl and add apples, onions, apricots, prunes, raisins. Sprinkle with salt and pepper. Mix. Stuff the goose with this mixture. Place the breast side up on a roasting pan.
Roast in a preheated 425F oven for 20 minutes. Reduce heat to 330F and roast for about 2 hours. To test doneness pricks the thigh. If the juices that run out are a pale yellow, the goose is completely cooked. Let stand 5 to 10 minutes before carving. Place on a large serving platter.
Serve with stuffing on the side.

DUCK BAKED WITH APPLES

1 whole duck, cut into 8 pieces
2 Tbsp sweet butter
2 large onions, halved and sliced
1 head of garlic, crushed
2 apples, cored and diced
2 tsp lemon juice
½ cup heavy cream
½ cup brandy
4 twigs cilantro
1 tsp salt
Pepper to taste
½ cup water

In a deep skillet, place the pieces of duck skin side down and fry over the moderate heat for about 10 minutes. Turn over and continue to fry until golden brown. Put the duck aside and take off excess fat from the skillet. Put the duck in the same skillet and pour brandy over it. Light the brandy for about a minute. The alcohol will evaporate and the duck will be left

with a light, special aroma. Take out the duck pieces from the skillet. In the same skillet heat the butter, add the onions and fry until golden brown. Add the apples, garlic, lemon juice, salt, pepper and water. Simmer for 15 minutes. Place the duck into a baking pan. Pour the prepared mixture over the duck. Cover with aluminum foil and bake in 330F oven for 30 minutes. Take the duck out of the oven, remove the aluminum foil. Pour heavy cream over the duck, cover again and put back into the oven for 30 minutes. Take off the aluminum foil and leave the duck in the oven for another 10 minutes.
Serve hot and garnish with twigs of cilantro.

BAKED SALMON

2 pound skinless salmon
2 Tbsp dill weed
1 onion sliced
2 Tbsp lemon juice
½ lemon sliced
3 Tbsp pomegranate syrup
Salt and freshly ground black pepper to taste

Rub the salmon with salt and pepper and let stand in refrigerator for 4 hours.
Place the salmon in a baking sheet, sprayed with cooking spray. Drizzle the fish with lemon juice, sprinkle the dill weed and put over sliced onions. Bake in preheated 400F oven for 25 minutes.
Serve hot with lemon slices and pomegranate syrup aside.

BOILED STURGEON

2 pounds sturgeon cut into 2- inch wide pieces
1 large onion, quartered
6 garlic cloves, peeled
A few twigs of dill and parsley, toughed
2 bay leaves
10 peppercorns
1 Tbsp salt
1 lemon, sliced

In a cooking pot bring 6 cups of water to boil. Add onions, garlic, dill, parsley, bay leaves, peppercorns and salt. Boil over the moderate heat for 20 minutes.
Add sturgeon pieces and cook for 20 minutes. Remove the sturgeon pieces with a slotted spoon; place them on a flat serving platter.
Serve hot with lemon slices.

BROILED STURGEN

2 pounds sturgeon cut into 3-inch pieces
5 twigs parsley, minced
1 onion, half sliced
½ cup pomegranate seeds
3 Tbsp pomegranate syrup (narsharab)
2 tsp salt
½ tsp freshly ground black pepper

Rub the sturgeon with salt and pepper. Let stand in a refrigerator overnight. The next day broil over the wooden charcoals until golden brown.
Push the fish from the skewers into a flat oval shape serving platter. Sprinkle over it the onions, parsley and pomegranate seeds.
Serve at once with pomegranate syrup and fresh vegetable salad.

GRILLED TROUT

1 large lake trout
3 garlic cloves
1 tsp lemon zest
2 Tbsp olive oil
2 tsp salt
½ tsp freshly ground black pepper

In a small bowl prepare the sauce from garlic, lemon zest, olive oil salt and pepper. Rub the trout with the sauce and let stand in a refrigerator for 3 hours. Wrap the fish into foil and grill for 30 minutes.
Serve hot.

BAKED BASS

1 large or small mouth bass
2 Tbsp lemon juice
3 Tbsp mayonnaise
2 tsp salt
½ tsp freshly ground black pepper

Rub the fish with salt and pepper. Line up the baking sheet with foil and spray with cooking oil.
Place the fish on foil and sprinkle over lemon juice and spread mayonnaise. Bake in 330F oven for 45 minutes.
Serve hot with white wine.

SHRIMPS FRIED WITH VEGETABLES

1 pound shrimps, cleaned
2 sweet onions, finely chopped
1 green bell pepper, finely chopped
1 red bell pepper, finely chopped
5 twigs cilantro, minced
3 Tbsp olive oil
¼ cup of any hot sauce for sea food
1 tsp salt

In a heavy skillet heat 1 tablespoon of olive oil and add the shrimps, sauce and salt. Fry covered over the moderate heat for 5 minutes.
In another skillet heat the remaining olive oil. Add peppers, onions and cilantro and stirring frequently fry until half cooked. Add this mixture to the shrimps and continuously mix for 5 minutes. Transfer into a serving platter.
Serve hot.

SHRIMPS WITH VEGETABLES AND RICE

1 pound shrimps, cleaned of skin
2 red bell peppers, diced
1 green bell peppers, diced

2 sweet onions, diced
2 Tbsp soy sauce
2 Tbsp olive oil
1 cup rice
2 tsp salt
Pinch of cayenne pepper
½ cup sweet butter
2 cups water

Wash the shrimps. In a heavy skillet heat olive oil and add the shrimps and salt. Cover, reduce the heat to medium and cook for 3 minutes. Set aside. Into the same skillet pour olive oil and put the onions and peppers. Fry over the moderate heat for 8 minutes. Add soy sauce, and cayenne pepper. Fry for 3 minutes, stirring frequently. Add the shrimps, toss well and remove immediately from the heat.
Meanwhile, in a cooking pot boil 2 cups of water. Add salt, butter and rice. Stir and cover. Simmer until rice is completely cooked.
Place the shrimps with vegetables and rice into a serving platter.
Serve hot.

5. MISCELLANEOUS

ONIONS SAUTÉ WITH EGGS AND TOMATOES

4 tomatoes, skinned, sliced
3 eggs, beaten
1 onion, finely chopped
2 Tbsp sweet butter
2 twigs cilantro, minced
Salt and pepper to taste

In a skillet melt the butter and add the onions and sauté until soft but not browned. Add tomatoes, sauté for 5 minutes. Sprinkle with salt and pepper to taste. Using a large fork beat the eggs with a pinch of salt and pour into the skillet. Cook about 5 minutes until the eggs are firm. Sprinkle cilantro and serve hot.

BROCCOLI WITH CHEESE

1 head broccoli, cut into pieces
½ pound mozzarella cheese
3 eggs, beaten
2 Tbsp olive oil
½ tsp salt
Pinch of nutmeg powder

Arrange the broccoli in one layer on a baking pan. Drizzle olive oil over it. Beat the eggs with nutmeg powder and salt. Arrange the mozzarella cheese over the layer of broccoli. Pour the eggs over the cheese. Bake in 375 F oven for 45 minutes. Turn off the oven and let stand for 3 minutes in the oven.
Serve hot.

STEAMED CAULIFLOWER

1 head cauliflower, rid of the core
½ tsp salt

Cut the cauliflower into a few pieces and place them into a strainer. In a deep pot boil three cups of water. Cover the strainer entirely and steam

about 20 minutes or until the cauliflower is tender but not overcooked. Transfer into a serving platter and sprinkle with salt.
Serve hot as a side dish with poultry or meats. If desired, sprinkle the cauliflower with apple cider vinegar.

BEETS IN ORANGE GLAZE

5 small beets, washed
2 Tbsp sweet butter
1/3 cup orange juice
2 tsp orange zest
1tsp sugar
½ tsp salt
¼ tsp freshly ground black pepper
2 twigs scallions, minced

In a cooking pot boil the beets over the moderate heat for 35 minutes. Cool the beets to room temperature. Cut into rings.
In a large skillet melt the butter. Add orange juice, orange zest, sugar, salt and pepper. Bring to a boil. Reduce the heat to low. Cover and cook for 10 minutes.
Add the beet rings and raise the heat so that the glaze boils. Cover and simmer for 5 minutes. Transfer into a serving platter. Sprinkle with minced scallions.
Serve hot or warm.

SIMMERED VEGETABLES

1 zucchini, sliced
1 red bell pepper, sliced
1 onion, cut half rings
2 tomatoes, peeled and sliced
½ bunch cilantro, minced
2 Tbsp olive oil
1 tsp salt
Pinch of freshly ground black pepper

In a skillet heat the oil. Add onions, zucchini, peppers and sauté stirring frequently for 5 minutes. Add the tomatoes, salt and black pepper. Cover and cook over the low heat for 15 minutes. Transfer into a serving platter, sprinkle with minced cilantro.
Serve hot.

GREEN BEANS FRIED

This dish is a Karabakh Armenians favorite.

2 pounds green beans, French cut
1 large onion, finely chopped
½ cup clarified or sweet butter
2 eggs
2 Tbsp water
½ bunch cilantro, minced
3 twigs purple basil
Salt to taste

In a heavy skillet melt the butter. Add the onions and sauté for 5 minutes. Add the beans, mix well and over the moderate heat, stirring frequently, cook until half cooked. Add salt, the water and cook until the beans are soft.
Beat the eggs with a fork or whisk and pour over the beans, mix well until the eggs are firm. Add cilantro and basil. Mix and remove from the heat. Cover and let stand for 10 minutes.
Serve hot with crispy homemade bread.

PUMPKIN STUFFED WITH DRIED FRUITS

1 medium sized pumpkin
1 cup rice, half cooked
½ cup apricots
½ cup dried cherries
½ cup raisins
1 Tbsp dried herbs
1 onion, chopped
½ cup sweet butter

1 tsp salt
Pinch of cayenne pepper

Cut the top of the pumpkin off and get rid of the insides. Cook the rice until half cooked and strain.
In a bowl, combine the rice, apricots, cherries, raisins, herbs, onions, salt and pepper. Pour the melted butter over the mix. Mix well and stuff the pumpkin.
Cover with the pumpkin top and put into the preheated 325F oven for 2 ½ hours.
Move the pumpkin into a flat large serving platter. Take the top off the pumpkin and slice the pumpkin vertically around the pumpkin until there is a circle left at the bottom and then open the slices like flower petals. Gather the stuffing like a small mountain in the middle of the pumpkin "flower".
Serve hot.

BAKED EGGPLANTS

3 eggplants, sliced into rings
5 large tomatoes, sliced into rings
5 garlic cloves, crushed
2 onions, cut half rings
1/3 cup olive oil
2 twigs cilantro, minced
2 twigs parsley, minced
Salt and pepper to taste

In a bowl pour hot water over the eggplants and drain.
In a baking sheet lay out tomatoes. Sprinkle salt. Put a layer of onions and garlic. Above all lay out a neat layer of eggplants. Sprinkle it with salt and pepper. Pour olive oil evenly over the entire surface.
Bake in the preheated 325F oven for 35 minutes.
With a spatula carefully transfer into a serving platter.
Garnish with cilantro and parsley.
Serve hot or cooled.

MEAT AND EGGPLANT STEW
("Ajib- Sandal ")

1 pound beef, cut into pieces
2 eggplants, peeled, sliced
2 onions, finely chopped
2 tomatoes, peeled, sliced
2 medium potatoes, sliced
½ bunch cilantro, minced
½ cup sweet butter
3 Tbsp water
2 tsp salt
½ tsp black pepper

In a bowl sprinkle the eggplant slices with salt and put them in a strainer for 1 hour. Wash under the cold running water, squeeze slightly to get rid of bitterness.
Wash the beef under cold water, squeeze well and put into a saucepan. Add the butter, cover and cook over the moderate heat, stirring periodically, until the meat is almost cooked. If needed, add a few tablespoons of water.
Add the onions, eggplants, tomatoes, potatoes, salt, and pepper. Mix well, cover and simmer for about 40 minutes until meat is completely cooked. Transfer into a deep serving platter and sprinkle with cilantro. Serve hot.

MUSHROOM JULIENNE

½ pound champignons, washed and chopped
½ pound mozzarella, grated
2 Tbsp sour cream
1 Tbsp heavy cream
1 Tbsp flour
1 tsp salt
Pinch of freshly ground black pepper

In a skillet place the mushrooms, cover and sauté for 5 minutes. Add the flour, cook over the moderate heat for 1 minute, stirring constantly, and add sour cream, heavy cream, salt and pepper.

Cover, reduce the heat to low and cook for two more minutes. Spoon the mushrooms into a small cup sized oven safe bowls. Sprinkle cheese over mushrooms and place the bowls on the baking sheet. Bake in a preheated 325F oven for 20 minutes.
Serve hot in the same bowls as cooked.

MUSHROOM CUTLETS

1 pound fresh mushrooms
1 onion, finely chopped
1 egg
3 Tbsp plain breadcrumbs
4 Tbsp all-purpose flour
3 twigs parsley, minced
3 Tbsp sweet butter
1 tsp salt

In a cooking pan bring the salted water to a boil. Add the mushrooms and cook for 3 minutes. Strain, cool and chop them.
 In a bowl combine the mushrooms, onions, egg, parsley, breadcrumbs and salt. Mix well.
In a heavy skillet, melt the butter. From the mixture make cutlets, roll in flour and fry on both sides until golden brown.
Serve hot with potato chips.

MUSHROOMS IN SOUR CREAM

1 pound mushrooms, any kind, chopped
½ cup sour cream
2 Tbsp melted butter
1 tsp all- purpose wheat flour
½ tsp salt

In a skillet melt the butter, add the mushrooms and fry for a few minutes, stirring frequently, over moderate heat. Sprinkle with salt and flour and add sour cream. Cook for 2-3 minutes and take off the heat.
Serve hot.

BOILED POTATOES WITH ONIONS

4 large potatoes, cooked, peeled
2 onions, finely chopped
3 Tbsp clarified butter
1 Tbsp dried herbs
1 tsp salt
1/3 tsp freshly ground black pepper

In a heavy skillet heat the butter. Add the onions and stirring frequently fry over the moderate heat until golden brown. Slightly mash the cooked potatoes and add to the onions.Sprinkle with salt, pepper and herbs. Mix well and fry together, stirring frequently, for about 5 minutes.
Serve hot.

FRIED POTATOES

4 large potatoes, peeled, cut into ½ inch strips
5 Tbsp clarified butter
1 tsp salt

In a bowl, sprinkle salt over the potatoes. Mix well.
In a heavy skillet heat the butter and put the potatoes there. Fry over the moderate heat, stirring often, for 5 minutes. Cover; stir periodically until they are golden. Lower the heat and cook for about 5 minutes until the potatoes are done.
Serve hot with pickles and fresh herbs on the side.

SIMMERED CABAGGE

1 pound white cabbage, sliced
1 large onion, sliced
2 Tbsp tomato paste
¼ cup sunflower oil
2 Tbsp water
Salt, pepper to taste

In a large nonstick skillet heat the oil. Add the onions and fry over the moderate heat for 5 minutes. Mix tomato paste with water and fry with onions for a few minutes more, stirring constantly. Add the cabbage, salt and pepper. Fry stirring a time to time until all liquid has evaporated and the cabbage turned light golden brown.
Serve hot. Also could be served as a side dish with meat, poultry and fish.

COTTAGE CHEESE BAKED

1 pound cottage cheese
2 Tbsp wheat cream
2 Tbsp sugar
2 Tbsp sour cream
½ cup raisins
1 egg
1 tsp vanilla
Pinch of salt

In a bowl combine cottage cheese, wheat cream, sugar, egg, raisins, vanilla and salt. Transfer into a baking pan. Spread sour cream over the entire surface and put into a preheated 350F oven for 30 minutes.
Take the baking pan from the oven, cool until warm. With a knife cut into middle size squares and serve with sour cream and strawberry syrup aside.

CREAMY WHEAT KASHA

3 Tbsp creamy wheat
½ cup milk
1/3 cup water
1 tsp sugar
¼ tsp salt
1 Tbsp melted butter

In a small pot mix milk and water, bring to boil. Reduce the heat to low. Add sugar, salt, creamy wheat and stirring constantly cook for 5-6 minutes. Add the butter, mix well.
Serve at once.

BUCKWHEAT KASHA

1 cup buckwheat, soak overnight with 1 cup water
1 onion, finely chopped
2 Tbsp sweet butter
Salt to taste

In a nonstick pot melt the butter; add onions and sauté for 5 minutes. Add the buckwheat and salt, mix, cover and cook over low heat for 15 minutes, stirring occasionally.
Serve hot.

RICE KASHA

1 cup rice, washed
1 cup milk
1 cup water
1 Tbsp sweet butter
1 tsp sugar
1 tsp salt

In a middle size pot pour the water and milk and bring to a boil. Reduce the heat to moderate and add salt, sugar and rice. Stir and cook until rice is tender. Remove from the heat, add the butter, mix and cover for 10 minutes. Serve hot.

GOLDEN WHEAT KASHA ("Khashil")

1½ cup hard wheat
2 large onions, finely chopped
½ cup clarified butter
2 tsp salt
½ cup yogurt
3 cups water

In a heavy skillet fry the wheat over the moderate heat, stirring constantly until golden brown. Ground the wheat or crack.

In a nonstick pot bring the water to a boil. Add salt, the wheat and stirring constantly cook over the moderate heat until cooked completely. Cover and set aside.
In a heavy skillet heat the butter, add the onions and fry over the moderate heat until golden.
Mix yogurt with 1/3 cup cold water. Add a pinch of salt.
Serve the kasha at once in deep serving plates, individually. Put the portion of kasha, make a hole in the middle of kasha and pour 1 tablespoon of caramelized onions with butter.
Surround the edges of kasha with yogurt mixture. It would taste better if spooning the kasha, onions with butter and the yogurt mixture at the same time.
Serve hot in the early morning, like Armenians do, as breakfast. Do not drink any cold liquids during and after this meal! Better have hot tea.

HOMEMADE COTTAGE CHEESE

4 cups whole milk
5 Tbsp sour cream

Mix ½ cup of milk with sour cream. Pour the mixture into remaining milk, stir well and cook in a nonstick cooking pot over the low heat for about 45 minutes or until it begins to boil and the clear liquid forms.
Remove from the heat, let stand for 10 minutes and strain. Place the prepared cottage cheese in a container, cover and refrigerate. Use within 4 days!

6. PILAFS

ARMENIAN PILAF WITH DRIED FRUITS

2 cups long-grain white rice (better use Basmati rice) soaked in slightly salted warm water for 1 hour
1 cup clarified butter
½ cup raisins, washed
½ cup prunes, washed
½ cup apricots, washed
½ cup of chestnuts, cleaned and cooked
1/3 cup flour
1 egg
5 tsp sugar
2 tsp salt

In a large heavy casserole bring to boil 6 cups of water. Add the rice and stir immediately. Cook over the high heat (do not stir anymore) until the rice is tender but still firm to the bite. Strain the rice and pour hot water over it. Drain well. Transfer into a large bowl. Sprinkle salt to taste and drizzle over ¾ cup of the melted butter. Using your hand and a large spoon, mix well. Keep warm.
In a small bowl whisk the egg. Sprinkle with a pinch of sugar, a pinch of salt and flour. Make the dough and roll it out into a thin circle same size as a bottom of a large cooking pot where the pilaf will be cooked. Cut the circle into 8 triangles and place them into the bottom of the pot and over the dough drizzle 1 tablespoon of melted butter. Fry on the both sides and leave on the bottom of pot. Add the rice. Gather the rice into a mountain and make several holes in it to get rid of the steam. Place a dish towel over the pot to absorb excess moisture. Put a lid and cook over the low heat for about 40 minutes.
When the pilaf is cooked, take off the towel, replace the lid and allow the pot stand in a warm place for 10 minutes before serving. Each individual grain of rice has to be on its own, that is producing a light and fluffy pilaf with a firm texture.
Meanwhile, in a heavy skillet melt 1 tablespoon butter. Add apricots, 2 tablespoons water and 2 teaspoons sugar. Cover and cook over the low heat until soft. Set aside.
In the same skillet add the remaining butter, prunes, raisins, 3 teaspoons of sugar and 3 tablespoon water. Cover and cook over the low heat for 5 minutes. Add the chestnut and apricots.

Cover and cook for 2-3 minutes more. Take off the lid and over the low heat, stirring constantly, fry all together until the liquid evaporates.
On a large flat serving platter mound the hot pilaf in a mountain. Place the sweet mixture over the surface of the rice. The crispy fried triangles from the bottom of the pot serve aside.
Serve at once.

PILAF WITH CARROTS AND ONIONS

½ pound lamb or beef, cut into pieces
½ cup cotton or sunflower oil
2 large onions , cut into half rings
4 medium carrots, cut into thin long strips
2 cups round rice, washed
1 head of garlic
2 tsp salt
½ tsp freshly ground black pepper

In a heavy skillet heat the oil. Add the meat and over the moderate heat fry until browned. Add ½ cup water, cover and cook until the meat is tender. Add the onions and stirring frequently fry for a few minutes and add the carrots. Constantly stirring, fry for about 10 minutes. Add 4 cups of water, salt, pepper and bring to a boil. Add the rice and cook uncovered until the water evaporates. Reduce the heat to low. Mound the rice, dip the head of the garlic deep inside, cover and simmer for about 35 minutes. Turn off the heat and let stand for 20 minutes until the rice is completely tender.
Serve pilaf hot in a deep serving platter with thinly sliced rings of red onions, seasoned with pinch of salt, pepper and 1 tablespoon wine vinegar.

VERMICELLI PILAF

1 cup vermicelli
½ stick sweet butter
1 medium size onion, diced
½ tsp salt
1½ cup hot water

In a heavy saucepan melt the butter. Add the onions and fry over the moderate heat until golden brown. Remove the onions from the saucepan.

In the same pan fry the vermicelli over the low heat, stirring constantly, until slightly brown. Add the fried onions, salt and pour the water over all.

With the saucepan partially covered, cook until the water evaporates. Mound the vermicelli, cover tightly, reduce the heat and cook for 15 minutes.

Serve hot as a side dish to meat or poultry dishes.

7. SAVORY PASTRIES AND PIES

CHEESE PASTRY I ("Khachapuri")

Dough:
4 Tbsp butter
1 tsp yeast
1 tsp sugar
2 eggs, beaten
½ tsp salt
1½ cup lukewarm water
4 cups sifted all-purpose flour

Filling:
1 pound cheese (salted mozzarella)
1 egg

For brushing:
1 egg, beaten

In a small bowl soften the yeast in 2 tablespoons of water. Let stand for 3 minutes. Add 1/2 cup of water, a pinch of sugar, a pinch of flour and stir well until the yeast has dissolved completely. Let stand for 5 minutes.
In a large bowl combine the flour, salt, yeast mixture, butter, eggs, the remaining sugar and water. Mix well, make the dough and knead on a floured surface until the dough is smooth and elastic.
Cover with clear plastic and a kitchen towel. Set aside in a warm place for 2 hours until the dough rises.
Meanwhile, prepare the filling: grate cheese and mix with egg.
Divide the dough into 10 equal pieces. Make the shape of a ball. Put them on a flat surface and cover with clear plastic and a kitchen towel. Let sit for about 15 minutes.
With a rolling pin roll out each piece into a 4-inch in diameter circle. Place 1 tablespoon of filling in the middle of each. Press the edges together to seal tightly making square shape pastries, leaving cheese open in the middle.
Arrange the pastries on the baking sheet. Brush the tops with a beaten egg and bake in a preheated 350F oven for 20 minutes or until golden brown. Place baked pastries on a flat serving platter.
Serve hot.

CHEESE PASTRY II ("Khachapuri")

Dough:
2 cup warm milk
1 tsp dry yeast
1 tsp salt
2 eggs
4 cups plus sifted all- purpose flour

Filling:
½ pound mozzarella, grated
½ pound feta cheese, grated
5 eggs

In a bowl mix 2 tablespoons of warm milk with the yeast. Stir and add the rest of the milk. Let stand for 10 minutes. In another bowl, whisk 2 eggs. Pour the yeast mixture into the eggs.
In a bowl mix the flour with salt and egg mixture. Using a large spoon mix well and then with the hands knead until everything is thoroughly blended. Shape the dough into a ball, brush with vegetable oil, place in a clean bowl, cover with a kitchen towel and put in a warm place for 45 minutes or until the dough rises.
Divide the dough into 5 equal pieces and shape into the balls. Roll out each ball into 12 inches wide in an oval shape and put on them the mixture of mozzarella and feta cheese. Roll the long edges twice so that the filling is visible, and pinch the short edges.
Bake in a 375F oven for 15 minutes. Remove from the oven. Break 1 egg over the visible part of each pastry and bake them for 15 minutes more or until the egg whites are completely cooked.
Serve at once.

CHEESE PASTRY III ("Khachapuri")

1 package puff pastry dough (good for 2 sheets of dough)

Stuffing
½ pound mozzarella cheese, grated
½ pound feta cheese, grated
1 egg

For top brushing:
1 egg, beaten

In a bowl, mix mozzarella and feta cheeses with egg.
On a flat surface roll out 1 sheet of dough, place half of it on ½ part of the baking sheet, so that other half of the dough is hanging over the edge of the baking sheet. Spread half of the cheese mixture over the dough sheet. Fold the hanging part of the dough over and pinch the edges together. Do the same with the remaining dough and filling on the same baking sheet . Brush with beaten egg. With a sharp knife score the upper layer of the dough into triangle shape pieces.
 Bake in a preheated 350F oven for 15 minutes. Take off the baking sheet from the oven. Cut with the same knife triangle shape pieces deeper to the base of the baking sheet. Put back to the oven and bake about 20 minutes until the tops of pastries are golden.
Serve at once.

CHEESE PASTRY IV ("Khachapuri")

Dough:
1 cup yogurt, warm
3 Tbsp sweet butter
1 egg,
1 tsp vinegar
½ tsp salt
Pinch of sugar
½ tsp baking soda
3 cups sifted all-purpose flour

Filling:
1 pound salted mozzarella, grated
1 egg

In a small bowl mix warmed yogurt with vinegar and baking soda. In a large bowl mix the flour with salt and sugar. Add the egg, yogurt mixture and butter. Mix well and make the dough. Shape it into a lump, cover with a kitchen towel and put in a warm place for 30 minutes.
Divide the dough into 2 equal parts. Shape the balls. Roll out on a flat surface one ball into a 10-inch circle. Mix the mozzarella and the egg and

put ½ of this mixture into the center of the circle. Pinch together the edges and flatten into a 12 inches in diameter circle. Press with the hands, flatten into 15 inches in diameter circle, turn over and put on a heated heavy skillet (no oil or butter!) and cook over the moderate heat until both sides are golden brown. Cut into triangle shape pieces, transfer into a serving platter.
Serve at once.

MEAT STUFFED PASTRIES I ("Belashi")

Dough:
2 Tbsp sour cream
1 tsp sugar
1 tsp active dry yeast
Pinch of salt
3 cup sifted all-purpose flour
1½ cup warm water

Stuffing:
2 pound ground beef
2 large onions, finely chopped
2 tsp salt
½ tsp freshly ground black pepper
2 Tbsp warm water

For frying:
½ cup corn oil

Sprinkle the yeast and sugar into ¼ cup of warm water in a small bowl. Let it stand for 3 minutes, then stir to dissolve the yeast completely. Put the mixture in a warm place for 5 to 10 minutes.
Pour the flour into a large mixing bowl and make a well in the center. Pour in the yeast mixture, sour cream, salt and remaining water. Make a dough and shape into a ball. Rub with olive oil, put into a clean bowl and cover with a kitchen towel. Place it in a warm, draft-free spot for 50 minutes or until the dough has doubled in volume.
In a mixing bowl put the meat. Add the onions, salt and pepper. Mix it with the hands and pour a tablespoon of warm water at a time and mix until blended.

Divide the dough into 25-30 pieces. Shape the balls, put them on a lightly floured surface and cover with a kitchen towel. Let them stand for 10 minutes. Press lightly to flatten the balls into 5 inches in diameter circles. Put the stuffing onto the balls. Pinch the sides together and let the stuffing still be seen in the middle. In a heavy skillet heat the oil and fry them over the moderate heat, face down first, and then turn over until both sides are a golden color.
Serve hot.

MEAT STUFFED PASTRIES II ("Piroshkies")

Dough:
1 pound lukewarm plain yogurt
2 Tbsp melted sweet butter
1 tsp baking soda
Pinch of salt
Pinch of sugar
4 ½ cups sifted all- purpose flour (approximately)

Filling:
1 pound beef, cooked, ground
1 large onion, finely chopped
1 Tbsp dried herbs (cilantro, basil, dill, mint)
1 tsp salt
½ tsp freshly ground black pepper
2 Tbsp corn oil

For frying:
1 cup corn oil

To make the dough, in a deep bowl combine the flour, salt and sugar. Make a well in the center. Mix the baking soda with yogurt and pour into the well. Add the butter as well and using a large wooden spoon, gradually mix until all the ingredients are well blended and the soft dough is formed.
Place the dough on a flat floured surface, knead well, put into a clean bowl, cover with a kitchen towel and let stand for 20 minutes. In a skillet heat the corn oil and add onions. Fry over the moderate heat, stirring frequently, until golden. Add the meat, dry herbs, salt and pepper. Mix

well and fry over the moderate heat for 3-4 minutes.
Cool to room temperature. Divide the dough into 20-25 small pieces. Shape the balls. Flatten them into 3 inches circles and put into each circle 1 tablespoon of the filling. Pinch the edges securely and between the hands make egg shape pastries.
In a heavy skillet heat the oil and when it is sizzling hot, place a few pastries and fry over the moderate heat until all sides are golden brown. Serve hot or warm.

MEAT STUFFED PASTRIES III ("Piroshkies")

Dough:
½ cup margarine, melted
2 eggs
1 cup warm yogurt
1 tsp dry yeast
¼ cup lukewarm water
1 tsp salt
Pinch of sugar
4 cups plus sifted all-purpose flour

Filling:
1 pound beef, cooked, ground
1 large onion, finely chopped
3 Tbsp sweet butter
2 Tbsp dry herbs
1 tsp salt
½ tsp freshly ground black pepper

For frying:
1 cup sunflower oil

Pour the lukewarm water into a small bowl and add the yeast. Let stand for 3 minutes and stir to dissolve the yeast completely.
In a deep bowl combine the flour, salt and sugar. Make a well in the center and pour the yeast mixture, yogurt, eggs and margarine. Using a large spoon, gradually blend the liquids into flour mixture, working from the center out. Beat until the ingredients are well blended and form soft dough.

Place the dough on a lightly floured surface and knead, sprinkling occasionally with just enough flour to keep it from sticking.

When it is smooth and elastic in texture, form into a lump and place in a lightly oiled bowl. Cover with clear plastic and a towel and leave to rise in a warm place about 2 hours or until doubled in size.

Meanwhile, in a heavy skillet melt the butter, add the onions and fry over the moderate heat until golden. Add the meat, dry herbs, salt and pepper and stirring frequently, fry for 5 minutes. Cool to room temperature.

Pinch down the dough and divide into 18-20 equal pieces. Form each into a ball and place on a lightly floured surface. Cover with a cloth and let stand about 20 minutes.

On a lightly floured surface roll out each of the balls into a flat circle approximately 3 inches in diameter. Place 1 tablespoon of the filling in the center of each circle, pinch the edges and between the hands make oval shape pastries.

In a heavy skillet heat the oil. When it is sizzling hot, place a few pastries and fry over moderate heat until all sides are golden brown.

Serve hot or warm with hot clear homemade beef broth (bullion) in large serving cups.

BAKED MEAT STUFFED PASTRIES ("Piroshkies")

Dough:
½ cup melted sweet butter
2 egg yolks
1 cup lukewarm plain yogurt
Pinch sugar
½ tsp salt
1 tsp baking soda
3 cups sifted all-purpose flour

Filling:
1 pound beef, cooked and ground
1 large onion, finely chopped
2 Tbsp sweet butter
2 egg whites
1 tsp dried herbs
Salt and pepper to taste

For top brushing:
1 egg, beaten

Pour the yogurt into a small bowl. Add baking soda and mix well. In a large bowl mix the flour with salt and sugar. Add the butter, egg yolks and pour in the yogurt mixture. Using a large spoon, mix until well blended. Place the dough in a lightly floured surface and knead thoroughly. When it is smooth and elastic, form into a lump and place in a lightly oiled bowl. Cover with clear plastic and put ina warm place for 1 hour.
Meanwhile, melt the butter in a skillet. Add the onions and sauté, stirring frequently until soft but not browned. Add the meat, and continue sauté for a few more minutes. Take the skillet from the heat and add salt, pepper, herbs and egg whites. Mix well and cool.
Divide the dough into 20 small balls. Roll out each ball into a circle about 3 inches in diameter. Place 1 tablespoon of the filling in the center of each circle. Pinch the edges tightly and shape into oval shape pastries. Brush with the egg. Place on a baking sheet and bake in a preheated 375F oven for 15-20 minutes or until golden brown.
Serve warm with light soups or homemade broth.

MEAT STUFFED PIE (in a puff pastry dough)

Dough:
¼ pound sweet butter
1 cup lukewarm yogurt
1 egg
1 tsp baking soda
½ tsp salt
1 Tbsp cold water
3 cups sifted all-purpose flour

Filling:
1 pound beef or turkey, cooked and ground
1 large onions, finely chopped
2 Tbsp sweet butter
1 egg
1 tsp salt
½ tsp freshly ground black pepper
½ cup pomegranate seeds

For top brushing:
1 egg, beaten

On a large cutting board sift the flour. Add salt, the butter and start to chop with a long knife until the small pieces of butter are covered with the flour. Add the egg, water and continue to chop.
In a small bowl mix yogurt with baking soda. Mix well and add into the flour mixture. Chop until the soft dough is formed. Roll out the dough on a lightly floured board and cut into 2 equal pieces and shape them into balls. Place them into a clean bowl, cover with clear plastic and put into the refrigerator for 30 minutes.
To make the filling, in a skillet melt the butter. Add the onions and sauté, stirring frequently, until lightly browned. Add the meat, salt, pepper stirring occasionally sauté for about 10 minutes. Take the skillet from the heat, add the egg, cool and mix with pomegranate seeds. Set aside.
On a lightly floured surface, roll out one ball into a ¼ inch thick sheet. Place it on a baking sheet. Spread the filling evenly, ¼ inches away from the edges. On the same surface, roll out the second ball into the same size as the first sheet. Place it over the feeling and press the edges together. Brush the surface with the beaten egg and make slight creases, horizontally and vertically in the dough, but do not cut all the way through. Prick down the entire surface and bake in a preheated 400F oven for about 15 minutes.
Take the sheet out from the oven and cut all the way through on the lines from before. Bake until lightly browned. Place in a serving platter.
Serve warm.

POTATOES STUFFED PASTRIES ("Piroshkies")

Dough:
½ cup margarine, melted
1 egg
1 cup lukewarm yogurt
2 tsp dry yeast
¼ cup warm water
1 tsp salt
Pinch of sugar
3 cups sifted all-purpose flour

Filling:
1 pound potatoes, cooked and mashed
2 large onions, finely chopped
1/3 cup melted butter
½ tsp salt
1/3 tsp freshly ground black pepper
1 Tbsp dried herbs

For frying:
1 cup sunflower oil

To make the dough, pour 2 tablespoon warm water into a small bowl and add the yeast. Let stand for 3 minutes, add the remaining water and stir to dissolve the yeast completely.
In a large bowl combine the flour, salt and sugar.
Make a well in the center and pour in the yeast mixture, margarine, egg and yogurt. Using a large spoon, gradually blend the liquids into the flour mixture, working from the center out. Beat until the ingredients are well blended. Place the dough in a lightly floured surface and knead thoroughly, sprinkling with flour occasionally to keep it from sticking. Form into a lump and place in a lightly oiled bowl. Cover loosely with a kitchen towel and let rise in a warm place until doubled in size.
Meanwhile, in a skillet melt the butter and add the onions. Sauté until golden brown, stirring frequently. Add the mashed potatoes, salt, pepper and dried herbs. Taste for seasoning, set aside and let cool.
Pinch down the dough and divide into 20 pieces and form each into a ball and place on a lightly floured surface. Cover with a cloth and let rest for 15 minutes.
On a lightly floured surface roll out each one of the balls into a circle 3 inches in diameter. Place 1 tablespoon of the filling in the center of each circle. Press the edges together and make with hands oval shape pastries. In a heavy skillet heat the sunflower oil and fry the pastries on both sides over the moderate heat until golden brown.
Serve warm.

MEAT STUFFED THIN PASTRIES (Kutabi)

Dough:
2 Tbsp corn oil

1 cup lukewarm water
1 tsp salt
2 cups sifted all-purpose flour

Filling:
½ pound beef, ground
2 onions, ground
½ tsp salt
1/6 tsp cayenne pepper powder

For brushing:
½ cup sweet butter

In a large bowl mix the flour with the salt. Add the oil and water. Using a large spoon gradually blend the liquids into the flour mixture, working from the center out. Beat until the soft dough is formed. Place the dough in a lightly floured surface and knead thoroughly until the dough is smooth and elastic in texture. Cover with a kitchen towel and let stand for 20min.
In a mixing bowl place the meat, ground onions, salt and pepper. Mix well. Press down the dough and cut into 12 pieces, forming them into balls and place on a lightly floured surface. Cover with a kitchen towel and let sit for 15 minutes. Roll out each ball into a circle 6 inches in diameter. Place 2 teaspoons of the filling on one half of each circle, spreading it evenly, about 1/6 inches from the edge. Fold over the other half to make a half circle and press the edges together.
Heat a heavy skillet (no oil!) and cook the pastries over the moderate heat until they are cooked on both sides. Brush both sides of the pastries with melted butter and place on a flat serving platter.
Serve hot.

CREPES I

Dough:
2 eggs
2 cups lukewarm milk
3 Tbsp melted sweet butter
1½ cup sifted all-purpose flour
½ tsp salt

In a bowl mix the flour with salt. Make a well in the center. Add the eggs and ½ cup of milk. Mix well, using a large spoon. Add the remaining milk, the butter and blend until smooth. Cover and let stand for 1 hour.
Take a skillet 8 or 9 inches in diameter, brush it with oil and heat over the moderate heat. Mix well the dough mixture and ladle a small portion of the mixture into the skillet and quickly rolling it, spread the mixture out evenly on the entire skillet and fry on both sides.
Serve at once with sour cream aside.

CREPES II

2 eggs
1 cup milk
5 Tbsp vegetable oil
1 Tbsp sugar
1 tsp salt
2 cups hot water
2 cups sifted all-purpose flour

In a large bowl mix the flour with sugar and salt. Add the oil, milk, eggs and mix it with a large spoon until well blended. Slowly add 2 cups of hot water, mixing quickly and beat until all the ingredients are well blended. Heat a medium size skillet, sprinkle with salt and when it is hot, take a napkin and wipe away the salt.
Heat the skillet for 30 more seconds. Spray the skillet lightly with cooking spray. Take the ladle and spread the mixture out evenly on the entire skillet. Cook one side until golden brown and then turn over, cooking the other side.
Transfer to a serving plate. Makes 25-30 thin crepes. With these crepes easy to make egg rolls with different fillings like mushrooms, meat or cottage cheese.
Serve warm with sour cream, jam or maple syrup.

MEAT STUFFED CREPES

Dough:
2 eggs

1 cup milk
5 Tbsp vegetable oil
1 tsp sugar
1 tsp salt
2 cups sifted all-purpose flour
2 cups hot water

Filling:
1 pound beef, cooked and ground
2 large onions, finely chopped
2 eggs, hard boiled, finely chopped
½ cup clarified butter
Salt and freshly ground black pepper to taste

In a large bowl mix the flour with salt and sugar. Add the oil, milk and mix with a large spoon until well blended. Slowly add hot water and mixing quickly beat until all the ingredients are well blended.
 Heat a medium size skillet, sprinkle lightly with salt and when it is hot take a napkin and wipe the salt away. Heat the skillet for more 30 seconds. Spray the skillet lightly with cooking spray. Take the ladle and rolling the skillet spread the mixture out evenly on the entire skillet. Cook one side until golden and then turn over, cooking the other side. Place them into a serving plate. Makes 25 -30 thin crepes.
In a heavy skillet, take ¼ cup of butter and heat over moderate heat. Add the onions and fry until golden brown. Add the meat, shopped eggs, salt and pepper. Mix well and fry for 3-5 minutes, stirring frequently.
On each crepe put 1½ tablespoon of the meat mixture . Roll into the shape of the rectangle. In a heavy skillet, heat the remaining butter and fry the stuffed crepes on both sides until golden brown. Arrange them on a flat serving platter. Serve hot with vegetable salad.

MUSHROOM STUFFED CREPES

Dough:
2 eggs
1 cup milk
5 Tbsp vegetable oil
1 Tbsp sugar
1 tsp salt

2 cups sifted all-purpose flour
2 cups hot water

Filling:
1 pound mushrooms
2 onions, finely chopped
1 tsp salt
1 Tbsp sour cream
2 Tbsp clarified butter

In a large bowl mix the flour with salt and sugar. Add the oil, milk, eggs and mix with a large spoon until well blended. Slowly add 2 cups of hot water and mix quickly. Beat until all the ingredients are well blended. Heat a medium size skillet, sprinkle with salt and when it is hot take a napkin and wipe away the salt. Heat the skillet for 30 seconds more. Spray the skillet lightly with cooking spray. Take the ladle and spread the mixture out evenly on the entire skillet. Cook one side until golden brown and then turn over and cook the other side. Place them into a flat serving platter. Makes 25-30 thin crepes.
In lightly salted water cook the mushrooms for 5 minutes and strain. Chop the mushrooms.
In a skillet heat the clarified butter. Add the onions and sauté until golden. Add the mushrooms, sour cream and salt. Fry together for about 5 minutes, stirring frequently. Let cool.
Put 1 tablespoon of the mushroom mixture onto each crepe. Roll into rectangles. In a heavy skillet heat the remaining butter and fry the stuffed crepes on both sides until golden.
Serve hot.

COTTAGE CHEESE STUFFED CREPES

Dough:
2 eggs
1 cup milk
5 Tbsp vegetable oil
1 Tbsp sugar
1 tsp salt
2 cups sifted all-purpose flour
2 cups hot water

Filling:
1 pound cottage cheese
2 Tbsp sugar
2 tsp vanilla
1 egg

For frying:
½ cup clarified butter

In a large bowl mix the flour with salt and sugar. Add the oil, milk, eggs and with a large spoon mix until well blended. Slowly add 2 cups of hot water and mix quickly. Beat until all the ingredients are well blended. Heat a medium size skillet, sprinkle lightly with salt and when it is hot, take a napkin and wipe away the salt. Heat the skillet for 30 more seconds. Spray the skillet lightly with cooking spray. Take the ladle and spread the mixture out evenly on the entire skillet. Cook one side until golden brown and then turn over and cook the other side. Makes 25-30 thin crepes.
In a bowl mix the cottage cheese, sugar, vanilla and egg.
In each crepe put 1 tablespoon of the cottage cheese mixture. Roll into the shape of the rectangles. In a heavy skillet heat the butter and fry on both sides until golden brown. Place on a flat serving platter.
Serve hot with sour cream on the side.

PLAIN PANCAKES

Dough:
1 cup plain warm yogurt
½ tsp baking soda
1 egg
1 Tbsp warm sour cream
1 tsp sugar
Pinch of salt
2 Tbsp corn oil
2 cups sifted all-purpose flour

For frying:
¼ cup corn oil

In a middle size mixing bowl combine yogurt, sour cream and baking soda. Mix well and add the egg, sugar, salt, and corn oil. Beat with a large spoon and add the flour. Beat for a few more minutes until well blended.
Heat a heavy skillet, pour some corn oil and when it begins to sizzle, put 1 tablespoon of the mixture onto the skillet (pour, at the same time, as many portions of the mixture as the size of the skillet permits). Fry both sides until golden brown. For the next portion add more oil and fry the remaining mixture.
Serve hot with jam, maple syrup or sour cream aside.

COTTAGE CHEESE PANCAKES

1 pound cottage cheese
1 egg
1 Tbsp sugar
3 Tbsp sweet butter
Pinch of salt
4 Tbsp sifted all-purpose flour

In a bowl using a large spoon mix the cottage cheese, egg, sugar and salt. Add the flour and mix well.
In a heavy skillet heat the butter. Spoon the mixture into the skillet, making about 2 inches in diameter pancakes. Fry over the moderate heat on both sides until golden brown.
Serve hot with sour cream aside.

WATER PASTRIES STUFFED WITH COTTAGE CHEESE

Dough:
1 egg
1 tsp salt
1 Tbsp melted butter
1½ cup lukewarm water
3 ½ cups sifted all-purpose flour

Filling:
1 pound cottage cheese
1 egg

2 Tbsp sugar

For brushing:
1/3 cup melted sweet butter

In a bowl mix the flour with salt. Add the butter, egg and water. Knead thoroughly until firm dough is formed. Divide the dough into 20 equal pieces and shape each into a ball. Place in a large pan, not touching one another. Cover with a damp cloth and let stand 30 minutes.
In a bowl mix the cottage cheese, egg and sugar.
On a lightly floured board, roll out each ball of dough into a 3 inch circle. Put 2 teaspoons of the cottage cheese into each circle, pinch the edges tightly, shape like a half moon.
In a large pot bring to boil 8 cups lightly salted water. Drop a few pastries into boiling water for 5-7 minutes or until they are floating. Take out with slatted spoon and place on a serving platter. Brush them with melted sweet butter. Do the same with the remaining pastries and put them on the serving platter over the first layer of the pastries and also brush them with the melted butter.
Serve hot.

WATER PASTRIES STUFFED WITH POTATOES

Dough:
1 egg
½ tsp salt
1 cup lukewarm water
2 ½ cup sifted all-purpose flour

Filling:
3 medium size potatoes, cooked, mashed
1 large onion, finely chopped
½ cup sweet butter, melted
Salt and pepper to taste

In a bowl combine the flour, salt, egg, water, and make a dough. Knead well, until smooth. Cover with a kitchen towel, let to rest for 30 minutes. Divide into small pieces, shape the balls. In the heavy skillet heat half of the butter, add the onions and over the moderate heat fry until golden

brown. In a bowl mix mashed potatoes with the fried onions, adding salt and pepper.
On a lightly floured board roll out each ball of dough into a 3 inch circle. Put 1 tablespoon of the potato mixture into each circle, pinch the edges tightly and shape like a half moon. In a large pot bring to boil 3 quarts of lightly salted water. Drop a few pastries into the boiling water for 5-7 minutes. Take them out, place in a serving platter, brush with the melted butter. Drop into the boiling water another portion of pastries. Boil and transfer them into the platter over the first layer of pastries. Brush with melted butter. Do the same with the remaining pastries.
Serve hot with green salad.

HERB STUFFED FLAT BREAD
("Zhengalov Haz")

Dough:
1 Tbsp sweet butter, melted
1 tsp salt
4 cups warm water
8 sifted all-purpose flour

Filling:
2 bunches cilantro
2 bunches chervil
1 bunch dill
1 bunch parsley
2 bunches scallions
1 bunch spinach
1 pound Swiss chard
½ bunch mint
1 bunch nettles
1 bunch sorrel
3 large onions, finely chopped
1 cup olive or sunflower oil
Salt, cayenne pepper and freshly ground black pepper to taste

Wash well all the herbs, drain and with paper towels get rid of the access water. Spread on a flat surface to dry for 45 minutes. Turn over, and dry for another 45 minutes. Chop the herbs and place into a very large bowl. Add the chopped onions and toss well.

In a large bowl mix the flour and salt. Make a well in the center, add the butter and water. Stir with a large spoon, working out from the center until gradually blended. Knead in the bowl until soft and elastic dough is formed, adding more flour if necessary. Shape into a ball. Place in a clean oiled bowl. Cover by plastic wrap, let rest for 30 minutes.

Punch down the dough and divide into 15 equal parts, and in a lightly floured surface shape each into the balls. Cover with a kitchen towels, let rest for 30 minutes.

Take 3 handfuls of herbs and put into a small bowl. Add salt, pepper and 3 tablespoons of oil. Mix well. (Do not mix all herbs with salt, pepper and oil).

Meanwhile heat a heavy large skillet. Roll out one ball into a circle 8 inches in diameter. Put one handful of the herb mixture into the circle. Raise the edges of the dough over the stuffing, tightly seal together and flatten into oval shape thin bread.

Transfer carefully with both hands the stuffed bread to the heated skillet. Fry over the moderate heat on both sides until golden brown. Place on a paper towels for a while and later cut in half and serve on a flat serving plate. When one is frying, prepare the next bread.

Serve hot.

JAM STUFFED TARTS

Dough:
¼ cup vegetable oil
1 egg
2 Tbsp sour cream
½ tsp dry yeast
5 Tbsp lukewarm water
Pinch of sugar
Pinch of salt
2 cups sifted all purpose flour

Filling:
½ cup apple jam

For frying:
½ cup corn oil

Combine the flour, salt, and sugar in a bowl. Make a well in the center and pour in the egg, oil and sour cream.
In a small bowl, dissolve the yeast in warm water. Pour the dissolved yeast into the well.
Working with a large spoon, stir the ingredients in the well and gradually stir them into the flour. Knead in the bowl or on a floured surface until the soft dough is formed. Shape into a ball and place into a clean and lightly oiled bowl. Cover with plastic wrap and a kitchen towel and let rise in a warm place, free from drafts for 2 or more hours, until doubled in size.
Punch down the dough. With lightly floured hands, take a small portion of the dough one at a time and make small balls. Put onto a lightly floured surface and cover with a damp cloth.
With the hands flatten the balls into circles 2 inches in diameter. Put in the middle ½ teaspoon of jam. Gather the edges and pinch to close. Shape into a ball.
In a small deep pot heat the oil. Drop into the oil a few balls. Fry over the moderate heat until golden brown.

8. BREADS

ARMENIAN HOMEMADE BREAD

2 Tbsp melted sweet butter
2 tsp active dry yeast
Pinch of sugar
½ Tbsp salt
4 cups sifted all-purpose flour
2 cups lukewarm water

For top brushing:
1 egg, beaten,
2 Tbsp sesame seeds

Sprinkle the yeast and sugar into ¼ cup of the lukewarm water in a small, shallow bowl. Let stand for 3 minutes and then stir to dissolve the yeast completely. Set the bowl aside in a warm spot for 10 minutes or until the mixture almost doubles in volume.
In a large bowl combine the flour, salt and sugar. Mix well. Make a well in the center. Pour in the yeast mixture, melted butter, and the remaining water. With a large spoon beat the flour into the liquid ingredients until thoroughly blended. Turn out the dough into a lightly floured surface and knead until smooth and spongy, sprinkling with a little flour if necessary to keep it from sticking.
Make a ball, put it into a clean large bowl, cover with clear plastic and a kitchen towel and place in a warm place free from drafts for about 2 hours or until it doubles in volume. Place the dough on a lightly floured surface and divide into 6 equal parts. Shape each part into a ball. Cover with a kitchen towel and let rest for 15 minutes.
Roll out each ball on a lightly floured surface, flattening into an oval so they are about 1-inch thick. Brush with eggs and with a sharp knife score each loaf with 2 diagonal lines and with fingers make holes between the lines and sprinkle lightly with sesame seeds. Place two loaves on a baking sheet. Let rise for about 20 minutes. Bake in a preheated 450F oven for about 20 minutes, or until the bread is golden. Transfer the breads to a wire cake rack. Bake the remaining dough balls similarly.

Second version of the recipe:
Divide the dough into 10 pieces, repeating the steps above. Roll out the dough 5inch in diameter and 1/3 inch thick. Bake in a preheated 400F oven for 13 minutes or until golden brown. Serve warm.

ARMENIAN THIN BREAD ("Lavash")

2 Tbsp melted sweet butter
1 tsp sugar
1 tsp active dry yeast
1 tsp salt
1 Tbsp vegetable oil
2 cups sifted all-purpose flour
½ cup wheat bran
1 cup plus 2 Tbsp lukewarm water

In a small bowl mix the yeast and sugar with ¼ cup warm water, stir well and let stand for 3 minutes. Stir, put in a warm spot and let stand for 10 minutes or until the mixture almost doubles in volume.
In a large bowl mix the flour, wheat bran with salt, make a well in the center and pour into it the yeast mixture, the remaining water and butter. Working with a large spoon, mix the flour into the liquid ingredients. Later, using your hands make dough in the bowl, kneading thoroughly. If needed, sprinkle more flour. Form a ball on a lightly floured surface. Oil the dough and transfer to a clean bowl. Cover with a kitchen towel and let stand in a warm place free of drafts for about 3 hours or until the dough almost doubles in volume.
Punch down the dough and divide into 12 equal parts. Shape balls, cover with a kitchen towel and set aside for 10 minutes. On a lightly floured surface roll out each ball as thinly as possible into circles. Prick the dough circles over the entire surface. Bake in a preheated oven at 400F about 20 minutes, or until the bread is pale golden brown. Repeat the rolling, pricking and baking procedure with the remaining balls. Cool the bread on a rack. Store in a tightly closed container. Serve as crackers. If you wish to have soft bread, 20 minutes before serving sprinkle the bread lightly with water and wrap in a kitchen towel to absorb the water. Thin bread is good with cheese and shish kebabs.

MULTIGRAIN BREAD

2 ½ cups sifted all purpose wheat flour
1 cup sifted rye flour
½ cup wheat bran
¼ cup oat bran

2 Tbsp flax seeds
1 Tbsp active dry yeast
½ tsp sugar
1 tsp salt
2 Tbsp melted butter
2 ½ cups lukewarm water

For brushing:
2 eggs, beaten

Pour the lukewarm water into a large mixing bowl. Sprinkle the yeast. Let stand for 5 minutes. Stir well to dissolve the yeast. Add 2 cups of wheat flour, sugar and salt. Using a large spoon stir well and let stand for 5 minutes. Add the butter, the rye flour, wheat bran, oat bran and flax seeds a little at a time and mix until smooth. Using your hands knead until elastic dough is formed and in a lightly floured surface form it into a ball. Place it into a lightly oiled bowl, turning, in order to grease the top. Cover with clear plastic and a kitchen towel, put in a warm place free from drafts about 3 hours or until it doubles in size. Punch down the dough and turn it over. Let stand for 30 minutes more. Punch down one more time and divide into 6 equal parts and shape each into a ball. Cover with a kitchen towel.
Roll out each ball into a ½ inches thick oval loaf and place 2 of them on a baking sheet.
Brush with the egg and using a sharp knife score two vertical lines over the top of the loaves. With your fingers make holes between the lines and let rise in a warm place for 20 minutes. Bake in a preheated 450F oven for 20 minutes or until golden brown. Cool them slightly on a cake rack. Do the same with the remaining balls of dough.
 Serve warm.

SWEET BREAD ROLLS

1½ cup lukewarm milk
½ cup sweet butter
2 Tbsp sugar
1 egg
1 Tsp brandy
1 Tbsp active dry yeast

4 cups sifted all-purpose flour

For brushing
1egg, beaten

In a large bowl pour ½ cup milk and sprinkle over the yeast and sugar. Mix and let stand for 5 minutes. Add the flour and make a well in the center. Add the butter, egg, brandy and milk.
Using a large spoon mix well from the center to the edges until the dough is firm. Cover well and let stand in a warm place without drafts for 1 hour or until the dough doubles in volume.
Divide the dough into 14-15 equal pieces and shape them into balls. Cover and let rest for 15 minutes. Slightly flatten the balls, place them on a baking sheet, brush with the beaten egg and bake in a preheated 375F oven for 20minutes or until golden. Serve warm.

9. DESSERTS

CAKE ("Karabakhi Kyata")

Dough:
2 cups lukewarm yogurt
3 egg
¼ cup sugar
1 cup melted butter
2 tsp active dry yeast
2 Tbsp warm milk
1 tsp vanilla
Pinch of salt
7 cups sifted all purpose flour

Filling:
 2 cups clarified butter
2 cups sugar
1 tsp vanilla
2 cups sifted all-purpose flour

For top brushing:
1 egg, beaten

In a bowl mix the yeast with the milk and let stand for 5 minutes. Stir to dissolve the yeast completely.
In a bowl combine the flour with sugar and salt and add into it all the liquid ingredients.
First working with a large spoon and later using the hands, knead thoroughly until soft dough is formed. On a lightly floured surface shape the dough into a ball and place in a large oiled bowl, turning over in order to grease the dough. Cover with a few kitchen towels and leave in a warm place free from drafts about 3 hours or until it doubles in volume.
Punch down the dough, turn over and let rise for 20 minutes more. Punch down again and divide into 4 equal parts and shape into balls.
Meanwhile, prepare the filling.
 In a mixing bowl beat the butter until its color turns white. Add   sugar and beat it for 3-5 minutes more. Add vanilla and the flour and mix until the mixture is smooth.
Place one ball at a time on a baking sheet and with the hands flatten the ball into a circle 10 inches in diameter. Put ¼ part of the filling into the center of the circle and pinch tightly the edges.

Turn over and flatten with the hands into a circle 12 inches in diameter. Brush with the egg and using a fork, score the top of the cake to make a design of diamonds and using the same fork, prick the surface to prevent it from expanding. Bake in a preheated 375F oven until golden brown about 30 minutes. Remove the cake from the baking sheet. Let it cool slightly on a rack.
Do the same with the remaining balls of dough and filling.
Cut the cake into triangle shape pieces and put them on a serving platter. Serve warm or cooled.
 Store in an airtight container.

BAKLAVA ("Bakinskaya")

Dough:
1 cup yogurt
3 eggs
½ pound margarine
1 tsp vanilla
3 ½ cup sifted all purpose flour

Filling:
1 pound walnuts, ground
1½ cup sugar
½ tsp cardamom powder
1 tsp vanilla

For decoration
35 walnut quarters

For brushing:
1 egg, beaten

On a board using a large knife cut the margarine into the flour until it is coated. Add the eggs and vanilla and continue cutting, add yogurt. Cut until the soft dough is formed. Divide into 5 equal pieces, shape into balls, cover with a kitchen towel and refrigerate for 20 minutes. On a lightly floured surface roll out one ball of dough into a thin rectangle, the size of the baking sheet. Transfer carefully to the baking sheet. Spread ¼ part of the filling over the dough sheet. Roll out the second ball of dough, place over the first layer and spread over the same portion of the filling. Do the same with the third and forth balls of dough and filling. Roll out the last, the fifth, ball of dough and put it over the forth layer of the filling. Press all the edges tightly and brush the top with the egg.

Using a knife, score the dough horizontally with 5 lines, then diagonally to make diamond shape pieces.

Decorate them by pressing lightly a quarter of a walnut into each diamond.

Bake in a preheated 325F oven for 20 minutes. Remove from the oven. Do not turn off the oven. Using a sharp knife, cut along the scored lines to the bottom of the baking sheet. Place the baking sheet back into the oven and bake for 40 minutes more. Remove the baking sheet from the oven and let stand for 10 minutes. Using a spatula place the "diamonds" on a flat serving platter.

Serve cooled.

WALNUT ROLLS ("Roulet")

Dough:
½ cup melted sweet butter
1 Tbsp lukewarm yogurt
1 cup lukewarm milk
2 eggs
1 tsp whiskey
1 Tbsp sugar
1 tsp vanilla
1 tsp active dry yeast
4 cups sifted all purpose flour

Filling:
¾ pound walnuts, ground
1 cup sugar
1 tsp vanilla
Top brushing:
1 egg, beaten

In a small bowl add 2 tablespoons of warm milk to the yeast stir and let stand for 3 minutes. Add the remaining milk and stir to dissolve the yeast completely. In a large bowl mix the flour with sugar and make a well in the center. Add the yeast mixture, yogurt, melted butter, eggs, vanilla and whiskey. Using a large spoon, blend the ingredients together to form soft dough. On a lightly floured surface knead until the dough is smooth and elastic. Place in a clean bowl, cover with clear plastic and a kitchen towel, wrap well with a warm blanket and put in a warm place free of drafts for about 3 hours or until it doubles in size.

Meanwhile, make the filling. In a bowl mix the walnuts with sugar and vanilla. Mix well and refrigerate for 1 hour.

Divide the dough into 4 equal pieces. Shape into balls, cover with a kitchen towel and leave to rise for 45 minutes. Roll out 1 ball thinly into a flat circle and spread ¼ part of the filling over it. Roll the dough with the filling loosely into a long roll and pinch the edges. Brush with the beaten egg. Prick all the way through the roll, in multiple places, to prevent it from expanding. Let sit for 20-30 minutes. Bake in a preheated 325F oven for 35 minutes or until golden. Let it cool on a cooling rack. Slice into ½ inches pieces widthwise.

Make the same with the remaining dough and filling.

Serve with hot tea or coffee.

WALNUT FILLED PASTRIES ("Badam- Buri")

Dough:
1 cup warmed sour cream
1 cup melted sweet butter
2 egg yolks
Pinch of sugar
Pinch of baking powder
½ tsp vanilla
3 ½ cups sifted all-purpose flour

Filling:
1 cup walnuts, ground
½ cup almonds, ground
¾ cup sugar
1 tsp vanilla

In a middle size bowl add to the flour the sour cream, mixed with baking powder. Add the egg yolks, butter, sugar and vanilla. Make dough and divide it into 2 pieces. Shape balls, cover with plastic wrap and put into a

refrigerator for 30 min. Mix the walnuts, almonds, vanilla and sugar. Put into a refrigerator for 20 minutes. Roll out the dough into circles 15 inches in diameter. Using a cookie cutter cut into circles, 2 inches in diameter. Put 1 full teaspoon of the filling. Holding a piece in one hand pinch the edges together making a moon shape pastry and with the first two fingers of the other hand make a curly pattern at the tautened edge. Bake in a preheated 350F oven for 20 minutes. Sprinkle the confectioners' sugar over the warm pastries.
Serve cooled.

CAKE "NAPOLEON"

Dough:
7 egg yolks
1 Tbsp sugar
1 Tbsp clarified butter
1 Tbsp vinegar
1 tsp vanilla
1 cup water
3 ½ cups sifted all purpose flour

Cream:
¾ pound sweet unsalted butter
1 can condensed milk (put into a refrigerator 5-6 hours before baking)
2 Tbsp brandy
1 tsp vanilla

For layering the dough:
¾ pound sweet butter, soft

In a middle size bowl mix the flour with sugar. Add the egg yolks, butter, vinegar, vanilla and water. Make a dough. It has to be stiff. Divide the dough into 5 equal pieces and shape each into a ball. Cover with clear plastic. Let rest for 30 minutes. Take one ball of the dough at a time and roll out on a lightly floured surface into a circle 14 or 15 inches in diameter. Avoid using a lot of flour, because the layers will not be light and crisp. Spread 1/10 part of the soft butter onto the entire surface of the dough. Fold the edges in the shape of a square. Cover with clear plastic, place into a refrigerator. Repeat the entire procedure with the remaining 4 balls of the dough.

Next, take from the refrigerator the first buttered dough square and roll out into a large rectangle Spread some butter over the entire surface, and fold the edges in the shape of a square. Cover with the same clear plastic and again put into the refrigerator. Do the same with the remaining squares.

Preheat the oven to 325F. Roll out one square of dough into the size and shape of a shallow baking sheet. Prick the entire surface of the dough with a fork. Bake for 20 minutes. Take out and carefully place on a cooling rack.

Bake the remaining pieces of dough on the same baking sheet, repeating the same procedure.

Meanwhile make the cream. Beat the butter in a mixer until it turns white. Still beating the butter, add the condensed milk in a very thin stream. Stop beating and add the brandy and vanilla. Beat a few minutes more until the cream is firm.

On a flat surface, take one of the layers and spread ¼ of the cream evenly. Then, put another layer over the first one and press lightly. Spread ¼ of the cream again, and put the third layer on and spread the cream. Do the same with the fourth layer. With a sharp knife shape the excess edges of the cake. Take the fifth layer of the cake and crush it into crumbs, sprinkling them over the entire surface of the top and edges. Sprinkle with confectioner's sugar. Move the cake carefully into a serving tray. Cover with clear plastic and refrigerate for about 2 hours.

Cut the cake into 2x3" rectangles and serve with hot tea.

SPECIAL SPONGY CAKE WITH CITRUS AND BERRY SYRUP

Dough:
8 eggs (brown)
1 ½ cup sugar
1 tsp vanilla
1 Tbsp cold water
1 ½ cup sifted all purpose flour

Cream:
¾ pound sweet unsalted butter
1 can condense milk (refrigerated overnight)
1 Tbsp brandy

1 tsp vanilla

Syrup:
½ cup sugar
½ cup water
2 Tbsp lemon juice
1/3 cup fresh black currant or strawberry juice
4 Tbsp brandy

Beat together the eggs and sugar until smooth and creamy. Add vanilla, water and beat for two more minutes. Add the flour, one tablespoon at time, into the cake mixture and using a large spoon, fold in the flour thoroughly after each addition.
Heat the oven to 225F. Butter and flour a deep 10- inch in diameter cake pan and line the bottom with wax paper. Pour the cake mixture into the prepared pan. Place into the oven and raise the temperature to 325F. Bake about 60 minutes or until the top turn's golden.
Caution: don't open the oven during the first 15 minutes. Cool for ½ hour before removing from the pan. Set aside to cool completely.
Meanwhile make the syrup. In a small saucepan combine sugar and water. Boil for 3-5 minutes. Cool. Add lemon juice, black currant or strawberry juice, brandy and stir.
Cut the cake into three equal layers. Take the crumbs from all the layers for cake decoration. Spoon 1/3 part of the syrup mixture over the first layer and spread 1/3 part of the cream. Repeat the same procedure with the other layers. Spread the cream over the sides of the cake. Sprinkle the crumbs over the top and the sides. Sprinkle with confectioners' sugar. Put into a refrigerator for about 2 hours before serving.

CURLY CAKE

Dough:
5 eggs
1 cup sugar
1 tsp vanilla
2 Tbsp cacao powder
1 cup cake flour
Cream:
½ pound soft sweet unsalted butter

½ cup sugar
¼ cup cake flour
¾ cup milk
1 tsp vanilla

Beat together the eggs, sugar and vanilla until stiff. Add the flour 1 tablespoon at a time, stirring well after each addition and using a large spoon fold into mixture.
 Butter and flour a 9-inch cake pan and line the bottom with waxed paper. Pour half of the cake mixture into the prepared pan and bake in a 325F oven for 30 minutes or until cooked. Cool for 30 minutes before removing from the pan. Set aside to cool completely.
Add the cacao powder to the remaining cake mixture, stir well and pour into the pan buttered and lined with wax paper. Bake in a 325F oven for 30 minutes or until cooked. Cool 30 minutes before removing from the pan. Set aside to cool completely.
Cut the cake into four equal layers. Carefully take the cake crumbs from the layers. Set aside the brown and yellow crumbs separately.
To make the cream mix ¼ cup of the cake flour with ½ cup of milk. Bring to a boil the remaining milk. Reduce the heat to low. Pour the flour mix into the milk and cook, stirring constantly, for 1-2 minutes. Cool and add the vanilla. Beat the butter it until turns white, add sugar, and beat for 5 minutes. Still beating, add the flour mixture. Beat a few minutes more until the mixture is light and fluffy.
 Spread the cream between the layers and on the top and sides of the cake. Sprinkle one half of the top with brown cake crumbs and the other half with yellow crumbs. Let it sit about an hour before serving.

LEMON CAKE

Dough:
1 cup sweet butter, soft
½ cup sour cream, warm
3 egg yolks
1 Tbsp sugar
½ tsp baking powder
1 tsp vanilla
3 cups sifted cake flour

Filling:
3 egg whites
¾ cup sugar
1 lemon grated
3 Tbsp strawberry jam or comfiture

In a bowl mix the flour with sugar. Make a hole. Mix the baking powder with sour cream and pour into the flour. Add the butter, egg yolks and vanilla. Using a large spoon, mix until it is smooth.
On a lightly floured surface knead the dough until it becomes elastic. Divide and shape into three equal balls. Cover and let stand for 10 minutes.
Roll out one ball at a time and line it up in a 9- inch cake pan. Bake in a 375F oven for about 20 minutes. Cool them. Slightly sprinkle warm milk on each of them. Take the crumbs from the edges.
 Beat together the egg whites and sugar until stiff. Mix the lemon with jam and fold in the egg mixture. Spread the filling between the layers, on the top and edges. Decorate with the cake crumbs.

CAKE "Bird's milk"

Dough:
3 eggs
½ melted margarine
3 Tbsp honey
1 tsp baking powder, mixed with 1 tsp vinegar
1 tsp vanilla
2 ½ cup sifted all-purpose flour

Filling:
¾ cup sweet butter
1 cup sugar
1 cup milk
4 Tbsp wheat cream
6 Tbsp lemon juice

Glaze:
1 Tbsp sweet butter
2 tsp cacao powder

2 Tbsp milk
2 Tbsp sugar

In a middle size bowl combine honey, eggs, butter, baking powder and vanilla and mix well. Add flour to the mixture 1 tablespoon at a time, stirring well after each addition until smooth dough is formed. Cut the dough into 4 equal pieces, shape balls. If needed, use more flour.
Roll out one ball into a thin circle, line up in an 9-inch cake pan and bake in a 325F oven for 20 minutes.
The same way bake the remaining balls. Cool them.
Meanwhile make the filling in a saucepan. Bring the milk to boil, reduce the heat to low and add creamy wheat. Stirring constantly cook for 4-5 minutes until smooth. Cool and add lemon juice.
Cream together the butter and sugar until light and fluffy. Slowly pour the wheat cream mixture and beat for 1-2 seconds.
In a small saucepan mix cacao with sugar. Add milk and cook over low heat, stirring constantly, until it boils. Add the butter and remove from the heat.
Spread the filling between the cake layers and pour the hot glaze on the top and sides of the cake. Set aside for 5-6 hours until all the layers are soaked and tender enough.

HONEY COFFEE CAKE

5 eggs
1 cup sugar
3 Tbsp melted honey
1 cup sweet butter
5 tsp instant coffee
1/3 cup hot water
1 tsp baking powder plus 1 tsp vinegar
2 cup sifted all-purpose flour

Beat together the eggs and sugar until light and creamy. Add 1 cup of flour, 1 tablespoon at a time and using a large spoon mix well.
Dissolve the coffee in hot water. Cool.
Mix coffee with honey, butter, baking powder and remaining flour. Fold in the beaten eggs mixture. Butter and flour 8-inch cake pan and line the bottom with wax pepper. Pour the cake mixture into the pan and bake in

a preheated 325F oven for 45 minutes. Cool the cake before removing from the pan. Cut the cake into thin slices.

CHERRY UPSIDE-DOWN CAKE

½ pound fresh pitted sour cherries
6 eggs
1 cup sugar
1 tsp vanilla
1 Tbsp cold water
1 Tbsp butter
1 cup cake flour

Beat together the eggs and sugar until light and creamy. Add vanilla, water and beat a few seconds more. Add the flour, 1 tablespoon at a time, stirring well after each addition and using a large spoon mix thoroughly.
Butter and flour a deep 8-inch cake pan. Line the bottom with buttered wax paper. Place cherries over the wax paper and pour the cake mixture over the cherries. Bake in 325F oven for 40 minutes or until cooked. Cool slightly before turning onto a serving dish. Sprinkle generously with confectioner's sugar.

APPLE PIE

2 pounds cooking apples
½ cup sweet butter
1 cup sugar
1 egg
½ cup walnuts, finally chopped
½ tsp cinnamon
1 cup sifted all-purpose flour

Peel, core and slice the apples. Place the apples in a buttered baking dish. Mix cinnamon with a pinch of sugar and sprinkle over the apples.
In a bowl mix the flour with sugar. Add the butter, egg and walnuts. Using a large spoon mix all together and spoon the mixture over the apples. Bake in a preheated 350F oven for 45 minutes.

Cool and serve the cake in the baking dish.

COTTAGE CHEESE PIE

1 pound cottage cheese
3 eggs, separated
1/3 cup sugar
½ cup cream wheat
1 tsp bread crumbs
1 Tbsp sweet butter
1 tsp lemon rind
1 pound fresh pears or fresh apricots
1 tsp vanilla

In a bowl beat the egg yolks until light yellow and foamy. Add the sugar to the egg yolks and beat again. Add cottage cheese, vanilla and mix.
Mix together cream wheat, lemon rinds and bread crumbs. Add into the cheese mixture.
Peel, core and slice the pears and add to the cheese mixture.
Beat the egg whites until stiff and fold into the mixture.
Butter and flour the baking dish and pour the mixture into it. Bake in a 300F oven until lightly golden. Serve in the baking dish.

MERINGUE PASTRY ("Beze")

3 egg whites
¾ cup fine sugar
Pinch of salt
Pinch of baking powder
1 tsp vanilla
1 tsp hot water

Beat the egg whites until stiff. Add 3 tablespoon sugar and continue to beat add baking powder, vanilla, salt, water and remaining sugar a little at a time and beat after each addition. Spoon the mixture into a buttered baking sheet. Bake in a preheated 250F oven for 90 minutes. Set aside to cool. Serve with fresh strawberries or raspberries. If desired, sandwich two meringues together by adding any cream between them.

CREAM PUFFS ("Eklers")

Dough:
½ cup sweet butter
4 eggs
Pinch of salt
1 cup sifted cake flour
1 cup water

In a saucepan combine the water, the butter and salt. Bring to a boil. Remove from the heat, add the flour and mix quickly and thoroughly. Return to the heat and cook over the moderate heat, stirring constantly, until thick and the mixture come away from the sides of the saucepan. Remove from the heat and cool until lukewarm.
Add the eggs one at a time beating well after each addition. Mix until smooth and shiny.
With a teaspoon take spoonfuls of the dough and put them on a baking sheet and bake in the preheated 400F oven for about 35 minutes. Cool and fill with any cream.

PASTRY "Roses"

Dough:
½ pound sweet butter, cool, grated
2 eggs
3 Tbsp sour cream
1 tsp baking soda plus 1 Tbsp vinegar
3 cup cake flour

Filling:
1 ½ cup walnuts, chopped
½ cup sugar
1 tsp vanilla

Over a bowl sift the flour and carefully fold in the butter. Add sour cream, eggs, baking soda plus vinegar and make a dough.
Mix the walnuts, sugar, vanilla and cool in a refrigerator for 30 minutes.
Cut the dough into five equal parts and shape into balls. Roll out the balls, spread the filling. Roll the dough with the filling into long rolls and using a

sharp knife cut into 1-inch pieces. Pinch one side of the pastries and place on a baking sheet, the pinched sides down. To give a shape of roses raise the middle circles of the dough and at the same time press down gently the other circles of the dough. Bake in a 325F oven for 25 minutes. Sprinkle generously with confectioners' sugar.

FLOUR HALVA

1 cup sugar
1 cup sweet unsalted butter
3 Tbsp whisky
2 Tbsp water
1 tsp vanilla
2 cups flour

Make a syrup in a middle size pot. Mix the water with sugar, bring to a boil, stirring constantly. Cool it, add vanilla and whisky.
In a heavy nonstick skillet melt the butter and add the flour. Cook over the low heat, stirring constantly until golden. Stir the syrup into the skillet and mix well with flour and butter. Remove from the heat, pour into a flat plate. Press quickly with a spoon into a thick square. Cut into small squares, cool them for an hour.
Serve with hot tea or coffee.

CHOCOLATE MOUSSE

½ cup bitter chocolate
1 Tbsp brandy
¾ cup heavy cream
1 Tbsp confectioners' sugar
Pinch nutmeg powder

Melt the chocolate in the top of a double boiler over very hot water. Add the brandy and mix.
Beat together heavy cream and sugar until the mixture is light and fluffy. Fold in chocolate mixture. Add nutmeg powder and place in a refrigerator for 2 hours before serving. Garnish with mint leaves.

JELL-O FRUIT SHOT

1 ½ Tbsp gelatin
½ cup fruit juice
½ cup vodka
1 cup hot water

Add the gelatin to the hot water; stir until the gelatin is dissolved. Add fruit juice, vodka, mix and pour into small glasses. Chill and serve.

CITRUS-BERRY JELL-O

1 cup sugar
1 Tbsp gelatin
1 tsp lemon juice
3 Tbsp raspberry or black currants juice
1 cup water

Soak the gelatin in boiled and cooled water about 2 hours. Pour out the excessive water.
In a small saucepan combine the sugar and water and bring to boil. Stirring constantly boil for 3 minutes. Remove from the heat, let stand until warm. Add the gelatin and stir well until the gelatin completely dissolves. Add raspberry juice and lemon juice. Stir well and pour the mixture into a deep square shape serving platter. Refrigerate 3 hours until firm. Before serving dip the bottom of the platter into warm water about 15 seconds. Cut into 1-inch squares and serve as dessert.

Note: The citrus-berry Jell-O can be used for cake decoration, if cooled slightly to drawling, lingering consistency and poured over the top and edges of cakes.

10. PRESERVES

SOUR CHERRY PRESERVE

2 pounds sour cherries
2 pounds sugar
½ cup water

Place the cherries in an enameled saucepan and sprinkle the sugar over them. Let stand for a few hours until juice is formed. Add the water and bring to boil. Reduce the heat to low and cook for 5 minutes. Remove from the heat and let stand until next day. Cook for 20-30 minutes over moderate heat, or until the liquid attains a medium-thick syrupy consistency. During the boiling skim off the foam as it rises to the surface. Cool.
Ladle into sterilized jars and seal.

WHITE CHERRY PRESERVE

2 pounds white cherries, pitted
1 ½ pounds sugar
½ cup water
2 Tbsp lemon juice

Place the cherries in an enameled saucepan and sprinkle the sugar over them. Let stand for a few hours until juice is formed. Add the water and bring to boil. Reduce the heat to low and cook for 5 minutes. Remove from the heat and let stand until next day.
Cook over the moderate heat for 25-30 minutes, or until the liquid attains a medium-thick syrupy consistency.
During the boiling skim off the foam as it rises to the surface. Cool and add lemon juice.
Ladle into sterilized jars and seal.

CORNELIAN CHERRY PRESERVE
("Hyuni muraba")

Cornelian cherry is a unique member of the Dogwood family. The fruit is similar to a tart cherry, ripens in late summer and Armenians use it in jellies, preserves and for wine making.

2 pounds cornelian cherries
2 pounds sugar
2 cups water

In an enameled saucepan combine sugar and water. Bring to boil, stirring constantly to dissolve the sugar. Add the cherries and remove from the heat. Cool. Bring to boil again and reduce the heat to moderate. Cook about 45 minutes or until the liquid attains a medium thick syrupy consistency. During cooking skim off the foam as it rises to the surface. Cool. Ladle the preserve into jars, cover and store in a cool place.

PLUM PRESERVE

2 pounds plums, pitted and poked
2 pounds sugar
2/3 cup water

In a enameled saucepan combine water and sugar. Bring to boil, stirring constantly to dissolve the sugar. Add the plums and remove from the heat. Let stand until next day. Bring to boil, reduce the heat to low and cook for 10 minutes. Set aside for 3 hours or until cool. Cook over the moderate heat for 15-20 minutes more. During the boiling skim off the foam as it rises to the surface. Remove from the heat and cool.
Ladle into sterilized jars and seal.

QUINCE PRESERVE

2 pounds quinces
2 pounds sugar
2½ cups water

Remove the core from the quinces, peel and cut into 1/2-inch slices. In a saucepan combine the water and sugar and stirring constantly bring to boil. Add the quince slices and reduce the heat to low. Cook for 5 minutes, remove from the heat and set aside for 5-6 hours. Cook again over the moderate heat until the fruit is tender and the liquid attains a light-thick syrupy consistency. During the boiling skim off the foam as it rises. Remove from the heat and cool. Ladle into sterilized jars and seal.

FIG PRESERVE

2 pounds figs, peeled and poked
2 pounds sugar
1 cup water
½ tsp vanilla

In a heavy saucepan combine the sugar and water. Bring to a boil, stirring constantly to dissolve the sugar. Add the figs. Reduce the heat to moderate, cook for 5 minutes and remove from the heat. Let stand for 5-6 hours. Bring to boil again, reduce the heat and cook over the moderate heat for 35-40 minutes or until the liquid attains a light-thick syrupy consistency. During the cooking skim off the foam as it rises to the surface.
Ladle into sterilized jars and seal.

STRAWBERRY PRESERVE

2 pounds ripe small size perfect strawberries
2 pounds sugar
3 Tbsp water

Hull, wash and drain the strawberries. Place them into a large saucepan and sprinkle sugar over them. Let stand overnight. Cook over the high heat about 2 minutes. Reduce the heat to moderate and cook for 15 minutes. Occasionally skim off the foam as it rises to the surface. Cool.
Ladle into sterilized jars and seal.

RASPBERRY PRESERVE

2 pounds raspberries
2 pounds sugar
3 Tbsp water
Place the raspberries in a large saucepan and sprinkle the sugar over them. Let stand overnight. Add the water and bring to boil. Reduce the heat to low. Cook for 20 minutes. Skim off the foam as it rises to the surface. Cool.
Ladle into sterilized jars and seal.

BLACK CURRANT PRESERVE

1 pound ripe black currants
1 pound sugar

Crush black currant berries in food processor, pour into a bowl and mix well with sugar. Let stand for a few hours.
Spoon into sterilized jars, cover and keep in refrigerator.

MARINETED GARLIC

2 pounds fresh garlic (just pulled up)
1 cup salt (plain)
2 Tbsp vinegar

Take the first two layers off the garlic heads and place them into a large jar. Fill the jar with cold water, and put in a sunny spot. Change the water every day. 4 days later dissolve 1 tablespoon salt in water and pour over the garlic. Place in a sunny spot.
On the 16th day almost all bitterness has to be gone. Wash the garlic under running water and place into small jars.
Pour into the jars enough water to cover the garlic completely. Pour the water from the jars into a bowl. Add 2 tablespoons of salt and 2 tablespoons of vinegar. Stir well to dissolve the salt. Pour over the garlic. Close the jars and refrigerate.

MARINATED EGGPLANTS

2 pounds small eggplants
1 bunch cilantro, chopped
½ bunch parsley, chopped
2 twigs dill, chopped
10 garlic cloves, finely chopped
3 Tbsp plain salt
2Tbsp sugar
3 Tbsp vine vinegar
2 cups boiled and cooled water

In a large saucepan bring to boil lightly salted water. Add the eggplants and boil for 3 minutes. Take the eggplants out and cool. Squeeze them and cut lengthwise.
Make a filling, mixing together garlic, cilantro, parsley and dill. Stuff the eggplants with the filling and place in a clean large bowl.
In a small bowl combine the salt, sugar, vinegar and cooled water. Pour over eggplants. Put over the press for about 12 hours.
Place the eggplants in the sterilized jars, pour the marinade over them, cover and store in a cool place.

MARINATED MUSHROOMS

2 pounds mushrooms
1 Tbsp salt
1 bay leaf
5 garlic cloves, finely chopped
2 Tbsp vinegar
3 cups water

In an enameled saucepan combine the salt and water. Bring to boil, stirring constantly to dissolve the salt. Add the mushrooms and boil for 3-5 minutes. Drain. Mix mushrooms with garlic, bay leaf and vinegar. Spoon the mushrooms into sterilized jars and seal.

ITALIAN GREEN PEPPER PRESERVE

2 pounds pepper, washed and poked
2Tbsp plain salt
½ tsp sugar
1 Tbsp vinegar
3 cups hot water

Leave the peppers in lightly salted cold water for 3 hours.
Pour the hot water into a bowl and add 1 tablespoon of salt and all of the sugar. Take the peppers out of cold water, squeeze and add to the hot mixture. Put over it a heavy press and let stand for 3 hours.
 Fill the jars with peppers. Add to the mixture the remaining salt, vinegar, stir well and pour over the peppers. Cover and store in a cool place.

CURED OLIVES

5 pounds fresh ripe black olives
3 pounds coarse salt
½ cup extra virgin olive oil

In a large bowl mix the olives and salt. Pour into a large sack and hang for 40 days until all the bitterness is gone. Wash well under running water and spread over a cotton sheet to dry. Pour olive oil into a large clean bowl, transfer the olives there and toss well. Fill the jars with the olives, cover and store in a cool place.

CABBAGE AND BEET PRESERVE

1 hard head of white cabbage, divided into 5-6 pieces
2 medium beets sliced
5 cloves garlic, minced
1 ½ Tbsp plain salt

In a large bowl place together the cabbage pieces, garlic and beet slices. Pour the salted water over it.
On top put a press for 3 days and keep in a warm place. Fill the jars and put in a refrigerator.

PRESERVED GRAPEVINE LEAVES

1 pound grapevine leaves
2 cups hot water
1 Tbsp plain salt

Take leaves that are young and tender. Remove the stems. Arrange in piles of 10-12. Begin from the stem ends and roll them into rolls.
Pack tightly into the sterilized jars, pour salted hot water over them and seal.

RED PEPPER PASTE PRESERVE ("Adjika")

5 red bell peppers, ground
15 garlic cloves, minced
1 ½ tsp salt
Pinch of cayenne pepper
2 tsp coriander powder
2 Tbsp Georgian spice "khmeli-suneli"
1 Tbsp vine vinegar

Over the high heat in a nonstick pot bring to boil the ground bell peppers. Reduce the heat to the moderate and cook, occasionally stirring, until all the liquid is almost gone. Add garlic, salt, pepper, coriander, "khmeli-suneli" and cook for 2-3 minutes longer. Remove from the heat and cool. Add vinegar, mix well.
Spoon into small sterilized jars and seal.

HORSERADISH SAUCE & MARINADE

¼ pound fresh horseradish, peeled, pureed
1 tsp sugar
1 tsp salt
1tsp beet juice
2 Tbsp vinegar
2 Tbsp hot water

Into a small bowl put the horseradish puree, add the hot water, cover and let stand until cool.
Add salt, sugar, beet juice, vinegar and mix well.
Spoon into small, sterilized jars and seal.

HOMEMADE MAYONNAISE

2 egg yolks
1 tsp mustard powder
1 tsp lemon juice
1 cup corn oil
½ tsp salt

Pinch of freshly ground black pepper
1 Tbsp warm water

Beat the egg yolks and salt. Add the mustard powder, the pepper and beat until pale yellow. By the drops add the lemon juice, corn oil and water. Beat for several minutes more until blended.
Spoon the mayonnaise into a jar, cover and refrigerate.

CLARIFIED BUTTER

2 pounds sweet butter
1 tsp salt
4 Tbsp water

In a heavy saucepan melt the butter over low heat and add the salt, the water and let boil for several minutes. Skim off the foam with a spoon as it rises to the surface.
 Remove from the heat and cool. Place in a refrigerator for 1 hour or until the butter is thick. Remove from the refrigerator, make a hole on the surface and drain the liquid. Carefully spoon the clear butter into a container, cover and store in a cool place.

11. USEFUL ADVICE AND PRACTICAL HINTS

1. The color of beef you are buying has to be not very dark. Look for meat with a light yellow vein. This kind of meat is more delicious and cooks faster.
2. The pork meat has to be light color, firm and without pellicles.
3. Buy lamb by the color of fat. If it is dark yellow, the animal was old.
4. For shish kebab use the meat of a lamb from the back legs and shoulder blades.
5. The young chickens have a light color of fat and a white color of skin.
6. For bullions use chickens with a rough skin and dark yellow fat.
7. Fish is fresh, if it has clear, bright eyes and shiny scales.
8. Before cooking the fish season it overnight with salt and pepper to taste.
9. Before cooking the meats and poultry soak them in lightly salted water for about 2 hours.
10. Marinade the meats, poultry and fish in glass or enameled bowls. To broil, for the best results, pat dry with paper towels.
11. Marinade the steaks using apple cider vinegar and no salt. Salt just before frying.
12. Before boiling eggs wash them under the running water and add a pinch of salt in the boiling water.
13. For the best results, use brown eggs to make sponge cakes.
14. Beaten egg whites and sugar mixture must be used right away.
15. While beating the egg whites add a pinch of salt.
16. For making dough use only wooden spoons.
17. Place an apple next to a sponge cake to prevent it from drying.
18. Before using saffron soak it in hot water for 20 minutes.
19. Potatoes keep their color if a few drops of lemon juice are added
20. to the boiling water.
21. To take the skin from tomatoes score with a sharp knife a cross on the top of tomatoes, drop them into boiling water for 30 seconds and then put into cold water and peel.
22. Salt the meats at the end of cooking.
23. While cooking a cauliflower, to avoid a smell, place next to the cooking pan a cup of vinegar. To keep whiteness, add into the boiling water a few drops of milk.

www.ingramcontent.com/pod-product-compliance
Lightning Source LLC
Chambersburg PA
CBHW071708040426
42446CB00011B/1973